HOW WALL STREET
FLEECES AMERICA

HOW WALL STREET FLEECES AMERICA

Privatized Banking
Government Collusion
and Class War

STEPHEN LENDMAN

CLARITY PRESS, INC.

ISBN: 0-9833539-4-8
   978-0-9833539-4-2

In-house editor: Diana G. Collier
Cover: R. Jordan P. Santos

Library of Congress Cataloging-in-Publication Data

Lendman, Stephen.
  How Wall Street fleeces America : privatized banking, government collusion and class war / by Stephen Lendman.
      p. cm.
  Includes bibliographical references and index.
 1. Federal Reserve banks. 2. Banks and banking--United States. 3. Finance--United States. 4. Monetary policy--United States. 5. United States--Economic policy. I. Title.
  HG2563.L46 2011
  332.10973--dc23

                              2011031817

Clarity Press, Inc.
Ste. 469, 3277 Roswell Rd. NE
Atlanta, GA. 30305 , USA
http://www.claritypress.com

Privatized banking let innovative Wall Street manipulators transform America into an unprecedented money-making racket, facilitated by government collusion at the highest federal, state and local levels.

For generations thereafter, working Americans have been scammed of their savings, jobs, homes and futures to let privileged elites get richer and more powerful.

This book is dedicated to working Americans and everyone who is for government of, by and for all the people, not just for the privileged few, rewarded generously at the expense of all others.

TABLE OF CONTENTS

1

DIRTY SECRETS OF
THE FEDERAL RESERVE

The US Federal Reserve, Bank of England, Bank of Japan and European Central Bank (for the 12 euro currency countries) have powers beyond what most people imagine. As a result, they and the Bank of International Settlements (BIS) control financial conditions everywhere in an increasingly borderless world where significant economic events in one nation affect others for better or worse.

Based in Basle, Switzerland, BIS is the central banker for central bankers, a banking boss of bosses accountable to no government. Moreover, it's privately owned by its members, the most powerful ones having most influence. Along with dominant central banks, financial elitists established it to control world economies globally, ideally with a single currency.

In his 1966 book, *Tragedy and Hope*, Professor Carroll Quigley said:

> [T]he powers of financial capitalism had another far-reaching aim, nothing less than to create a world system of financial control in private hands able to dominate the political system of each country and the economy of the world as a whole. This system was to be controlled in a feudalist fashion by the central banks of the world acting in concert, by secret agreements arrived at in frequent private meetings and conferences.[1]

Their scheme is close to fulfillment unless public outrage stops them. They plan global control of money, credit and debt to be able to dominate economies, politics, commerce, and military adventures, so that these might be conducted in a way that benefits them advantageously.

In fact, the power to create money can build or destroy nations. In private hands, it goes to the root of today's problems. More on that below.

America's Federal Reserve is most dominant, but it wasn't always that way, and today it has top spot competition it hadn't experienced since WW II. Established in 1913, the Fed has existed for nearly a century, its dominant members today running America like their private fiefdom.

In contrast, the Bank of England was established in 1694 as a private institution to provide funds to the government. In 1844, the Bank Charter Act gave it sole Royal Charter right to issue notes and coins. In 1946, it was nationalized. Then in 1997, it again was given operational independence over monetary policy. The 1998 Bank of England Act Part II mandates its responsibilities and objectives, including its authority to set interest rates. The Bank's website states:

> As a public organization, wholly-owned by Government, and with a significant public policy role, the Bank is accountable to Parliament.

In addition, its entire capital is held by the Treasury solicitor on behalf of HM's Treasury. However, the Bank functions like a private institution even though it's not.

The Fed's 1910 Jekyll Island Creation

In 1910, seven powerful men met secretly for nine days on Jekyll Island, creating the Federal Reserve System. It was then established by Congress three years later on December 23, 1913. Thereafter, the American and world economies were changed, aiding mostly rich and powerful beneficiaries. The law might not have passed if it hadn't been carefully shepherded through the December 22, 1913 Congressional Conference Committee meeting which took place from 1:30 - 4:30 AM when most members of Congress were sleeping. The next day, the Act passed with many legislators away for the holiday break, while most in town hadn't read it. It didn't matter. Its language was carefully crafted to deceive, concealing the empowerment of private banks to control the nation's money, their long sought after goal.

Their idea worked as planned even though the Federal Reserve Act is illegal under the Constitution's Article 1, Section 8, giving Congress sole power to coin (create) money and regulate the value thereof. In 1935, the US Supreme Court ruled that Congress can't constitutionally delegate its authority to another group or body. Legislators thus acted unconstitutionally by establishing a private for-profit corporation engaged in exploiting the public welfare. As a result, the lawmakers defrauded the public, but got away with it because who would stop them, especially when presidents go along, as Woodrow Wilson did by signing the act.

Wilson later admitted his mistake, saying:

I am a most unhappy man. I have unwittingly ruined my country. A great industrial nation is controlled by its credit system. Our system of credit is concentrated. The growth of the nation, therefore, and all our activities are in the hands of a few men. We have come to be one of the worst ruled, one of the most completely controlled and dominated Governments in the civilized world, no longer a Government by free opinion, no longer a Government by conviction and the vote of the majority, but a Government by the opinion and duress of a small group of dominant men.

Wilson was also responsible for signing the Espionage Act of 1917 and Sedition Act of 1918, banning public opposition to America's WW I participation. The Sedition Act specifically prohibited use of "disloyal, profane, scurrilous, or abusive language" (free speech) about the government, flag, or military policy. It applied only when America went to war, legally or otherwise, then was repealed in December 1920.

Wilson also authorized the Palmer Raids in 1919 and 1920 against union activists, alleged radicals, and so-called anarchists during the Red Scare, the first anti-communist crusade. The second was from 1947-1957, when Joe McCarthy ruined the careers of many innocent victims, a tradition kept active by extremist congressional members and administrations today, who have no qualms about scapegoating and exploiting people for political advantage.

Under Wilson and McCarthy, the enemy was communism and the result was the Cold War. Today, it's militant Islam and the bogus "war on terror." The scheme: heighten fear to justify repression at home and imperial adventurism abroad, always at the public's expense.

In the past decade, under the pretext of humanitarian intervention, Iraq, Afghanistan and now Libya have been victimized by naked aggression, launched to replace one regime with another more pliable one, control their resources, exploit their people, privatize state industries under Western (mainly US) control, and establish new Pentagon bases to be used for greater regional dominance, to prevent any democratic spark from emerging. Fed-created money provides generous financing.

In his day, Wilson began it by letting private bankers control money, which they have done for nearly a century now. On June 4, 1963, perhaps with the intent to end it, Jack Kennedy signed Executive Order (EO) 11110 to:

- amend EO 10289 (dated September 17, 1951) which empowered the Treasury to perform certain designated "functions of the President without the approval, ratification, or other action of the President;" and

- thereby perhaps bypass the Fed and empower the president to issue currency; it constitutionally authorized the federal government to create and "issue silver certificates against any silver bullion, silver, or standard silver dollars in the Treasury."

Though not verified, some believe Kennedy then ordered the Treasury Secretary to issue nearly $4.3 billion worth of United States notes, perhaps to replace Federal Reserve Notes. Whether or not he wanted the Federal Reserve System ended (thereby returning money creation power to Congress as the Constitution mandates) is speculation, but perhaps fear of it and more, led to his assassination five months later.

In late 1963, after Johnson became president, US notes were withdrawn from circulation. In 1964, Johnson said: "Silver has become too valuable to be used as money." Respected Fed critic and author of *The Creature from Jekyll Island*, G. Edward Griffin, wrote:

> There was a third point, however, which everyone seemed to overlook. The Executive Order 11110 did not instruct the Treasury to issue Silver Certificates. It merely authorized it to do so if the occasion should arise. The occasion never arose. The last issuance of Silver Certificates was in 1957... six years before the Kennedy [EO]. In 1987, [it] was rescinded by [EO] 12608, signed by Ronald Reagan.[2]

Without mentioning EO 11110, Reagan did it by amending EO 10289, rescinding the Treasury's right to issue silver-backed notes.

Back in 1910, the original plotters against the US currency met on Jekyll Island. They represented some of the world's richest, most powerful figures—the Morgans, Rockefellers, Rothschilds (dominating European banking by the mid-1800s, becoming the wealthiest, most influential family worldwide) and others.

Among them was a US senator, a high ranking Treasury official, the president of the nation's then largest bank, a leading Wall Street figure, and the man who later became the Fed's first chairman. It was a powerful group who had come together for one purpose—to subvert constitutional law for ongoing self-enrichment and secret control. Thereafter, oligarchy and monopoly replaced marketplace competition, which was dominated by money power.

Baron M.A. Rothschild's maxim, "Give me control over a nation's currency and I care not who makes its laws", was carried out. They also knew Proverbs 22:7, stating: "The rich rule over the poor, and the borrower is servant to the lender."

A new era dawned, the age of powerful cartels, after the seven financial titans had colluded not to compete. Today, America's Wall Street-headquartered banking cartel controls the nation's money, giving it virtually limitless power. Working cooperatively with governments and corporate allies, they control world markets, resources, and cheap labor, exploiting them for maximum profits.

The Federal Reserve System: Money Power in Private Hands

The Federal Reserve functions as follows:

Composed of a Board of Governors in Washington and 12 major city-located regional banks throughout the country, the Fed includes numerous member banks. All national banks, in fact, must be part of the system. Others could join and many did.

In November 1914, the Federal Reserve began operating, mandated by law to have the greatest of all powers—the power to create and control the nation's money, credit and debt. Few people understand the process or its importance.

Under the Federal Reserve Act, Fed banks in each region are owned by their members—the larger the bank, the greater the equity. They're all private, unrelated to government, operating like other businesses with stockholders paid 6% interest annually on their capital and surplus. Half that amount is repaid to their Reserve Bank. The Board of Governors can call in the other half.

Their holdings represent a legal obligation of Fed membership. Their stock may not be sold or pledged as collateral for loans, nor bought by individuals or entities other than member banks.

With the power to create money, the Fed finances its own operations without congressional funding, remitting its net income to the Treasury.

Besides domestic members, owners include powerful foreign investors in Britain, France, Germany, The Netherlands and Italy. They're partners with giant US banks like JP Morgan Chase, Citibank, Bank of America, Wells Fargo and Goldman Sachs, comprising a powerful banking cartel affecting global business and everyone's lives.

This private ownership has been challenged several times in federal courts—to no avail. The current system under which each Fed Bank is a separate corporation owned by commercial banks in its region has always been upheld.

One such challenge was *Lewis v. United States*, leading to the 9th Circuit Court of Appeals ruling that Fed banks are independent, privately owned and locally controlled corporations.

America's Founding Fathers Differed With Powerful Bankers

Our founding fathers knew how the Bank of England had exploited America's economy under Britain's Currency Act, prohibiting the colonies from issuing their own money. That had turned prosperity into poverty by halving their money supplies.

According to Benjamin Franklin, it was this that caused America's Revolution. It wasn't over tea taxes or other issues. It was over poverty, unemployment and exploitation, the proximate sparks for many uprisings, notably similar to those today in the Middle East, with people wanting jobs, better wages, essential benefits, and governments serving them, and not monied interests.

Most Founders also knew the danger of letting bankers accumulate too much wealth and power. James Madison called them "Money Changers," saying:

> History records that the Money Changers have used every form of abuse, intrigue, deceit and violent means possible to maintain their control over governments by controlling money and its issuance.

Thomas Jefferson explained:

> I sincerely believe that banking institutions are more dangerous to our liberties than standing armies. Already they have raised up a money aristocracy that has set the government at defiance. The issuing power should be taken from the banks and restored to the people to whom it properly belongs.

Jefferson and Madison understood commercial monopoly dangers. In fact, they unsuccessfully tried to prevent them by proposing two additional "Bill of Rights" amendments.

To assure liberty, they wanted constitutionally-mandated "freedom from monopolies in commerce" (which has led to today's corporate giants, including major Wall Street banks) and "freedom from a permanent military," or standing armies. Had they succeeded, today's America might look entirely different.

Their failure caused great harm because government relinquished its money creation power, which in turn facilitated militarism and the growth of standing armies, used today for global imperial dominance.

Before his assassination, Abraham Lincoln notably said the following:

> The money powers prey upon the nation in times of peace
> and conspire against it in times of adversity. It is more
> despotic than a monarch, more insolent than autocracy
> and more selfish than a bureaucracy. It denounces, as
> public enemies, all who question its methods or throw
> light upon its crimes. I have two great enemies, the
> Southern Army in front of me and the bankers in the rear.
> Of the two, the one at the rear is my greatest foe.

Though unconfirmed, he has been cited as also having said:

> I see in the near future a crisis approaching that unnerves
> me and causes me to tremble for the safety of my
> country ... corporations have been enthroned and an era
> of corruption in high places will follow, and the money
> power of the country will endeavor to prolong its reign
> by working upon the prejudices of the people until all
> wealth is aggregated in a few hands and the Republic is
> destroyed.[3]

Imagine what he, Jefferson or Madison would say today. Or Andrew Jackson who called the Bank of the United States a hydra-headed monster, entrapping nations in debt, and refused to renew its charter. Notably he called bankers "...a den of vipers and thieves", adding, "I intend to rout you out, and by the grace of the eternal God, I will rout you out."

Lincoln's sentiment may have cost him his life. International bankers despised him after Congress passed the 1862 Legal Tender Act, empowering the Treasury to issue paper money called "greenbacks" interest free after Lincoln refused to pay bankers the usurious 24-36% interest rates they demanded on loans he needed to wage war with the South.

After his death, a new banking law was passed. The Greenback law was rescinded, once again requiring the government to pay interest on its own money. It's an outrageous fraud, but it's law.

How the Federal Reserve System Works

After Congress and President Wilson privatized the nation's money system, the government's exclusive right was relinquished. The law was so outrageous that the Fed had to be designed to look federal, concealing its control by powerful profiteers headquartered on Wall Street—hence, the name, Federal Reserve.

Its member banks share in the vast profits, earned from having the most valued of all franchises—the right to print money, control its supply and price, and benefit hugely by loaning it out for profit, including to the government, which is then forced to pay interest on its own money, a payment it could avoid by creating money on its own.

Lincoln ducked it successfully by issuing greenbacks. So did colonists for 25 years of sustained, inflation-free, tax-free growth and prosperity. Then they lost it by ceding control to the Bank of England.

Mechanics of Fed Operations

The Fed operates in three ways:

> 1. through open market operations;
> 2. by the discount rate it charges member banks; and
> 3. by establishing member bank reserve requirements to be held, not loaned out.

The Board of Governors decides the discount rate and reserve requirement, while the Federal Open Market Committee (FOMC) runs market operations involved in buying or selling bonds. Using these tools, the Fed influences the supply and demand for money, thus directly controlling the federal funds' short-term rate that's always fixed unless the Fed raises or lowers it.

Market forces control longer rates, though this is greatly influenced by powerful institutional traders manipulating values advantageously—a topic addressed later in the book.

The FOMC and How It Works

The Federal Open Market Committee is key to the whole money creation/contraction process. It consists of 12 members—seven from the Board of Governors, the president of the New York Fed Bank (the dominant mother bank) and four of the remaining 11 Reserve Bank presidents who serve one year terms on a rotating basis.

The FOMC holds eight regularly scheduled meetings annually to assess economic conditions and decide how to loosen or tighten monetary policy in whichever way it wants, ostensibly to achieve sustainable growth and price stability. In fact, it has other aims—benefitting banking giants at the expense of popular needs and maintaining high unemployment, a large reserve army of labor that will keep wages and benefits restrained. Their agenda is very much part of today's Main Street depression, created by destructive Fed policy, and driven by member bank greed.

The FOMC literally creates money out of thin air in a four step process:

Step 1. The FOMC first approves purchase of US government bonds on the open market.

Step 2. The New York Federal Bank buys them from sellers. Financial markets always need an equal number of both.

Step 3. The Fed pays for its purchases with electronic credits to the sellers' banks, which, in turn, credit the sellers' bank accounts, literally creating money out of thin air.

Step 4. Banks receiving credits then use them as reserves to loan out as much as 10 times their amount (if their reserve requirement is 10%) through the magic of fractional reserve banking.

This explains how it serves as an economic growth engine when Fed policy is expansive. When contraction is planned, the above process is reversed. Instead of buying bonds, the Fed sells them to move money out of buyers' accounts instead of into them, thereby reducing banks' reserves. Bank loans must then be reduced tenfold if the reserve requirement is 10%.

How the Fed Harms Public Welfare

The Federal Reserve System benefits its owners and member banks at the expense of working households by letting major banks restrict competition for greater profits. As a result, people lose out four ways:

1. **From inflation's invisible tax**, caused by diluting purchasing power by newly created money reducing the value of the dollars in circulation. The Greenspan and Bernanke Feds have been especially expansive yet have never been held to account. As a result, future generations will inherit enormous problems they created to benefit the wealth and power interests they serve, at the public's expense.

Greenspan became Fed chairman in August 1987. From 1982 until 1992, money supply growth averaged 8% a year. However, from 1992-2002, it exceeded 12% annually, and post-9/11, it reached 15%, having more than doubled in less than a decade.

After becoming Fed chairman in February 2006, Bernanke initially slowed money supply growth and raised short-term interest rates, but not for long, especially after September 2008 when massive expansion of the money supply began. By March 2010, the nation's monetary base had grown from $850 billion to $2.1 trillion in a period of 18 months, expanding more than two and a half fold, the greatest increase in US history. And it didn't stop.

As a result, the federal deficit exploded. Money creation continues, and future interest rates will rise.

In early 2002, before he became Fed chairman, Bernanke gave a speech titled, "Deflation: Making Sure It Doesn't Happen Here," saying, "... the US government has a technology, called a printing press [or today, its electronic equivalent] that allows it to produce as many US dollars as it wishes at essentially no cost." He referred to economist Milton Friedman's statement about using a "helicopter (money) drop" to prevent deflation. Thereafter, critics called him "Helicopter Ben," a derisive term, chiding him for reckless monetary expansion, potentially threatening serious future inflation.

However, economist Michael Hudson believes hyperinflation is unlikely, saying every instance "in history stems from the foreign exchange markets. It stems from governments trying to throw enough of their currency on the market to pay their foreign debts," owed in creditor currencies, not their own. But America can issue bonds to service its debt obligations. Moreover, the Fed can create money to buy them in unlimited amounts.

Currencies, however, may also be manipulated as a way of waging war by other means, to crush economies for advantageous exploitation, the way the Asian tigers were in the late 1990s, opening them to Western predators.

Chapter 5 discusses quantitative easing, whether it's an elixir or poison. It's the former if properly used. Bernanke hasn't done so, yet very much knows how. It's not rocket science. It's simple sound economics, discussed later in the book. Instead, Bernanke focused on rescuing Wall Street, fueling speculation, and growing world equity valuations (the stock market) at the expense of sustainable growth.

As a result, future economists will regard the Greenspan/Bernanke period as the most irresponsible in Fed history. It's a powerful reason for returning money creation power to Congress where it belongs. More on that topic ahead.

2. **The Fed also practices usury** by controlling short-term interest rates, moving them up or down to any level it wishes. When high, small borrowers face hurdles that larger borrowers can better withstand. If the Fed were practicing sound money low inflation policies, it would be able to keep costs low and benefit all borrowers equally.

3. Wilson endorsed the 1913 Federal Revenue Act imposing an **income tax in order to be able to pay bankers interest on government debt** in lieu of Congress creating money interest-free. As a result, a portion of working households' tax money pays tribute to Wall Street. The larger the deficit, the greater the burden, especially as inflation-adjusted for future generations.

Con artists couldn't have conceived a greater scam. Why else would some observers call America's economy a giant ponzi scheme, stealing from the poor and middle class for the rich.

Speaking from prison, convicted ponzi investor Bernie Madoff expressed the same sentiment to *New York* magazine. In a February 27, 2011 published interview, he called the "whole new regulatory reform a joke," expressing disdain for financial industry members and complicit regulators, who are regularly fleecing investors out of billions of dollars.

He should know. He did it for decades until his house of cards collapsed, which is the potential threat the entire economy faces, perhaps sooner than imagined.

A century ago, Henry Ford once said, "It is well enough that people of the nation do not understand our banking and monetary system, for if they did, I believe there would be a revolution before tomorrow morning." Today's scam is infinitely greater, yet public ignorance perpetuates it.

People literally don't know a Wall Street/government cabal is robbing them, transferring their wealth to powerful banks, other financial industry beneficiaries, and America's super-rich. It's the world's greatest ever racket, protected by the full faith and credit of Washington under both parties.

Why else would corporate profits be at record levels while Main Street remains mired in depression, ravaged by high unemployment, growing poverty, hunger and homelessness, exacerbated by millions of foreclosures and planned austerity when massive stimulus is needed? Helicopter Ben has given little to beleaguered households, states, or local communities. Neither has Washington.

4. Compounding other abuses, Wall Street also gets **public tax money in bailouts** whenever too-big-to-fail banks need financial help to survive. As do corporate favorites like General Motors, General Electric, hedge fund Long-Term Capital Management in 1998, and others. But not small banks, businesses, or working households, which are left on their own to sink or swim.

Adam Smith's Likely Reaction to Today's Federal Reserve

Concentrated power operates the opposite of Smith's *Wealth of Nations* ideology, where the market is described as working much like an "invisible hand", working best with many small businesses competing locally against each other. He opposed concentrated mercantilism, the equivalent of today's concentrated corporatism, able to restrict competition, maintain high prices, and earn greater profits at the public's expense.

Smith would have condemned today's system, run privately by the

Fed for its own self-enrichment, instead of using a nationalized central bank to foster sustainable inflation-free long-term growth—just what privately controlled money power prevents.

Another Way the Fed Harms the Public

Ostensibly the Fed was established to stabilize the economy, smooth out the business cycle, maintain healthy sustainable growth, and contain inflation, thereby benefitting everyone. Its record shows otherwise.

Since 1913, the economy has lurched from one crisis to another, including the crashes of 1921 and 1929, followed by the Great Depression until WW II. Post-war, other recessions followed in 1953, 1957, 1969, 1975, 1981, 1990, 2001, and 2007. Inflation bouts were also experienced, beginning in the late 1960s, then exacerbated through much of the 1970s and 1980s.

Moreover, hundreds of savings and loan banks failed during the 1980s banking crisis, the most ever in US history until currently, which is promising to far surpass the S & L crisis before ending. Financial deregulation was at fault both times, removing government oversight, thus licensing banks' willful fraud through financing speculative risks, which no bank should be allowed to do.

The 1980s, however, were just a preview of today's new millennium crisis, ravaging millions globally, and devastating Main Street America, now in the early stages of depression. The worst is yet to come, yet official policy discounts it, claiming we are witnessing improving economic growth. Repetition perpetuates these myths. This one's heard daily but rings hollow in suffering working households, struggling to survive.

On the eve of the 1929 market crash, famed economist Irving Fisher said, "Stock prices have reached what looks like a permanently high plateau." Instead they lost 89% of their value before stabilizing, then needed 25 years to regain full value. Perhaps a similar tragedy awaits today's investors once artificial stimulus runs out.

Besides permanent instability, you can also blame the Fed also for:

- soaring consumer debt;

- record federal budget and trade deficits;

- record levels of personal bankruptcies and home foreclosures;

- crushing future generation debt burdens;

- industrial America's decline by off-shoring high-paying/good benefits jobs to low wage countries;

- an 80% service economy, providing mostly low-paying, low-skill jobs with few or no benefits; and

- unprecedented concentration of wealth in fewer hands at the expense of middle and lower income earners.

Complicit with government, the Fed abused popular interests to benefit America's aristocracy. Replacing it with public banks is more essential than ever. Chapter 17 discusses the benefits. The time is now, the name of the game fairness—which can't exist under privately controlled money. For nearly a century, that constitency has gotten away with the grandest of grand thefts.

Owning a bank is the best way to rob one. Preventing it requires ending the private bankers' franchise, achieved and maintained by colluding with Washington to loot the federal Treasury and American households.

Returning money creating power to Congress, as well as creating state and local public banks will foster sustainable economic growth, prevent inflation, lower taxes, and produce enormous universal benefits, including employment for everyone able to work.

Business cycle instability will end. Money costs will be cheap. Too-big-to-fail banks won't exist. Wall Street's franchise will be rescinded. Sustainable money creation will spur growth. Ponzi scheme economics will end. Democratic values will be restored. An unimaginable new society will emerge, benefitting many, not the privileged few. Achieving it starts with reclaiming public money creation power. More on how, later in the book.

Endnotes

1   Carroll Quigley, *Tragedy & Hope: A History of the World in Our Time*, Angriff pr., 1975.

2   Edward Griffin, *The Creature from Jekyll Island: A Second Look at the Federal Reserve*, American Media, 1998, p. 569.

3   Supposedly written in reference to the passage of the National Banking Act of 1863 less than five months before he was assassinated in a letter to one Col. William F. Elkins, referenced in Emanuel Hertz's 1931 book, *Abraham Lincoln: A New Portrait*. Found on p. 40 of *The Lincoln Encyclopedia*, by Archer H. Shaw (Macmillan, 1950, NY), and Jack London's, book *Iron Heel* (1908). see <http://www.snopes.com/quotes/lincoln.asp>

2

CAPITALISM AND FREEDOM UNMASKED

On November 16, 2006, an era ended when economist Milton Friedman died. A torrent of eulogies followed. The *Wall Street Journal* mourned his loss with the same tribute Friedman had credulously used when Ronald Reagan passed, saying "few people in human history have contributed more to the achievement of human freedom"—this about a president responsible for massive human misery. More myth than man, Reagan's lawless, scandal-plagued tenure deserved condemnation, not praise.

Neither was Friedman's true legacy exposed. Economist and former Treasury Secretary Lawrence Summers called him a hero and "Great Liberator" in a *New York Times* op-ed. The *Financial Times* said he was "the last of the great economists." Terence Corcoran, editor of Canada's *National Post*, mourned the "free markets'" loss of "their last lion," and Bloomberg's *BusinessWeek* magazine noted the "Death of a Giant," praising his doctrine that "the best thing government can do is supply the economy with the money it needs and stand aside."[1]

Rarely has so much undeserving praise been given to anyone in light of the human wreckage their legacy left behind.

Friedman believed government's sole function is "to protect our freedom both from [outside] enemies...and from our fellow-citizens." The purpose of government is to "preserve law and order [as well as] enforce private contracts, [safeguard private property and] foster competitive markets." Everything else in public hands is socialism, or in other words, for free-wheeling market fundamentalists, is blasphemy.

Friedman said markets work best unfettered of rules, regulations, onerous taxes, trade barriers, "entrenched interests" and human interference, and the best government is practically none at all, as anything it can do, private business does better.

Democracy and government of, by and for the people? Indeed blasphemy, as private money control would be subverted, creating impediments for profiteering and plunder.

Friedman and his acolytes said public wealth should be in private hands, the accumulation of profits unrestrained, corporate taxes abolished, and social services curtailed or ended. He believed "economic freedom is an end to itself...and an indispensable means toward [achieving] political freedom."[2]

He found state laws requiring licensing for occupations (like doctors) a restriction of freedom. He opposed foreign aid, subsidies, import quotas and tariffs as well as drug laws, which he called a subsidy to organized crime. He ignored how profitable the drug trade is for Wall Street banks, which benefit hugely from money laundering.

He favored a constitutional amendment requiring that Congress balance the budget because deficits "encourage political irresponsibility." He claimed taxes were onerous and favored "cutting [taxes] under any circumstances and for any excuse, for any reason, whenever possible..." and exempting corporations entirely.

He opposed the minimum wage, supported a flat tax for the rich, and believed everyone should have to buy medical insurance like any other product or service, whether or not they can afford it.

He opposed public education, supported school vouchers for privately-run schools, and believed marketplace competition improves school performance, even though voucher amounts are inadequate and mostly go to religious schools, violating America's church-state firewall.

Friedman denounced unions, calling them "of little importance [historically in advancing] worker [rights and gains] in the United States," when, in fact, none existed until union struggles won them.

He also claimed "the gains that strong unions win for their members are primarily at the expense of other workers [and believing otherwise] is a fundamental source of misunderstanding." For him, supply and demand fundamentalism asserted that "the higher the price of anything, the less... people will...buy." Thus, he contended:

> Make labor of any kind more expensive and the number of jobs of that kind will be fewer. Make carpenters more expensive, and fewer houses...will be built [and those constructed will] use materials and methods requiring less carpentry. Raise the wages of airline pilots [and] there will be fewer jobs for them [because] air travel will [cost more and] fewer people will fly.

Friedman's bottom line: high union wages harm everyone, including rank and file members. They raise prices, lower demand, and destroy jobs, he believed, and thoughtlessly embraced the contrary, arguing that underpaying wages creates prosperity. But this was for the elite few alone, not the many he disdained.

He also opposed Social Security, calling it "The Biggest Ponzi Scheme on Earth" in an article with that title.[3] He described today's system as:

> an unholy combination of two items: a flat-rate tax on earnings up to a maximum with no exemption and a benefit program that awards subsidies that have...no relation to need [forgetting it's our most successful poverty-reducing program] but are based on [criteria like] marital status, longevity and recent earnings.

Friedman wanted it privatized, abhorred the "tyranny of the status quo," and agreed with Barry Goldwater that it be voluntary which, of course, would kill it. He added:

> [It's] hard to justify requiring 100% of the people to adopt a government-prescribed straitjacket to avoid encouraging a few [in fact, many millions] 'lower-income individuals to make no provision for their old age deliberately [even though most cannot], knowing they would receive the means-tested amount.'

Addressing only eligible retirees, he ignored millions of others who are dependent on Social Security, including disabled workers as well as spouses and children of the deceased, retired or disabled. These comprise around 37% of recipients, are left out of Friedman's calculation, and would get nothing under an easily manipulated privatized system able to destroy assured government benefits, an issue Friedman ignored.

For Friedman, we're on our own, "free to choose." But we're unequally matched against corporate predators and America's aristocracy, which assures that national prosperity accrues solely to them. Less privileged, the rest of us are hamstrung under Friedman's 1962 *Capitalism and Freedom*'s manifesto, saying: "To each according to what he and the instruments he owns produces." In other words, everyone's on their own, sink or swim, with his brave new world leaving human wreckage everywhere.

He opposed market-interfering democracy, an egalitarian society, government provision of essential services, workers' freedom from bosses, citizens from dictatorship, and countries from colonialism. Instead, he espoused economic freedom as a be-all-and-end-all, calling limited government and profit-making the essence of democracy, the best of his possible worlds.

Friedman's Chicago School Fundamentalism

Raised in New York, Friedman got his BA at Rutgers, an MA at the University of Chicago, and his doctorate at Columbia. Surprisingly, he espoused Keynesianism early on, but Friedrich Hayek's teachings changed him into a free market fundamentalist whose prominence would cause so much harm.

In 1946, he returned to the University of Chicago's Economics Department, becoming its charismatic missionary to revolutionize his profession and world economies—for the worse, not better.

His core doctrine was simple. Free-wheeling capitalism works best, especially when actual or perceived crises occur. These present opportunities for reactionary changes not possible at other times, making what was once impossible inevitable—permanent "reforms" like privatizing public schools or ending collective bargaining.

Friedman and his colleagues tried proving it mathematically through computer models showing markets are magical. He believed that unfettered, they produce the right amount of products and services, at the right prices, by the right number of workers, earning the right amount of wages to buy what's produced.

In short, a win-win for everyone—paradise. Or is it? In fact, it's voodoo science, sounding good but incompatible with democracy. Friedman and his "Chicago Boys" believed otherwise, but needed a controlled laboratory to prove it—economies following his diktats.

This led to many hellish models: in Chile under Augusto Pinochet, then Argentina, Uruguay, Bolivia, Brazil, Central America, China, Russia, South Africa, Eastern Europe, Sri Lanka, elsewhere in Asia, Israel, and America since the late 1970s.

Friedman believed that the ends justify the means, that repression is acceptable to pursue them, and that free choice offered "more room for individual initiative...a private sphere of life [and a greater] chance [that the authoritarian regimes he supported would facilitate, then] return to a democratic society." How, he didn't explain.

He countered critics by saying "economic freedom is an essential requisite for political freedom," transition pain a fair price for an eventual free market paradise. He and Hayek called social democracy, collectivism, socialism, and welfare state economics the "road to serfdom," producing "bondage and misery," and "coercion rather than freedom."

It was hokum, but who could prevail over Friedman's powerful market fundamentalist backers, including supportive media and academic ideologues. On the ground, it was different, with unfettered capitalism leaving human wreckage everywhere.

The Human Toll

Every free market state suffered—not their elitists, just ordinary people who were exploited for profit in pursuit of "economic freedom." Early on, Friedman's dogma was considered quirky, on the margins of mainstream economics, and out of step with the Keynesian post-war golden age that lasted until the 1970s when recession, stagflation and high unemployment changed everything.

Keynesianism was unfairly blamed, and it gave Friedman his chance to prove unfettered markets work best.

Chile: The First Test Case Under Pinochet

The results were disastrous. Chileans to this day are still affected by the September 11, 1973 coup that transformed Latin America's most vibrant democracy to despotism.

Friedman's playbook promised paradise but delivered "Caravan of Death" justice,[4] hyperinflation, economic decline, lower wages, fewer benefits, 20% unemployment, shattered unionism, gutted social services, severe poverty, ghostly factories, rotting infrastructure, out-of-control corruption and cronyism, all of which led to a massive transfer of public resources to private hands, with a repressive military and secret police targeting dissenters with detention, torture and death.

It was hell for Chileans, but nirvana for its aristocracy and foreign investors, who were profiting handsomely from public wealth transfers to themselves. It was just the beginning. Friedman's "shock treatment" moved on to more targets.

One of many was Bolivia with predictable results, leaving Friedman unrepentant. Food subsidies were ended, social services gutted, price controls lifted, wages frozen, oil prices hiked 300%, spending cuts imposed, unrestricted imports allowed, and state-owned companies downsized, costing hundreds of thousands of jobs before they were privatized.

Moreover, real wages dropped 40%, poverty soared, but a privileged elite got rich. Public anger grew. Repression followed, including the use of tanks against strikers, and police targeting union hall dissenters, universities and factories. Friedman-style "freedom" produced hell before getting worse.

Post-Communist Russia

It was tragic, not triumphant. In March 1985, Mikhail Gorbachev assumed power, planning political and social change, but he wasn't around long enough to lead it. He liberalized the country, introduced elections, and favored a Scandinavian-style social democracy, combining free market capitalism with strong social safety net protections. He envisioned "a socialist beacon for all mankind," an egalitarian society. But he never had the chance to built it.

When Soviet Russia dissolved, Gorbachev was out. Boris Yeltsin became Russia's president, supporting a corporatist state following the Chicago School "shock therapy" masquerading as "reform." Former apparatchiks became "nouveaux billionaires" ("oligarchs"), off-shoring the country's wealth to safe tax havens.

Russia's people were devastated:

- 80% of Russian farmers went bankrupt.

- 70,000 state factories closed, causing an unemployment epidemic.

- 74 million Russians (half the population) became impoverished; for 37 million, conditions were desperate, and the country's underclass remained permanent.

- Alcohol, painkilling and hard drug use soared.

- HIV/AIDS became epidemic with over a 20-fold increase since 1995.

- Suicides rose dramatically, and violent crime increased more than fourfold.

- Russia's population declined by around 700,000 a year before stabilizing; in the 1990s, unfettered capitalism had destroyed it at an alarming rate.

It's a startling condemnation of Chicago School orthodoxy, and the man who triumphantly spread it in the name of a freedom that's fake, ferocious, destructive and fatal.

Post-Soviet States

Free market shock therapy devastated the post-Soviet states, lowering, not raising, living standards. Poland was one of its victims. In the 1980s, Solidarnosc (Solidarity) unionized 10 million members, gaining the right to bargain and aspiring to transform state-controlled companies into worker-run cooperatives. Instead, mines, shipyards and factories were privatized, subsidies slashed, and price controls lifted. Far worse times than before resulted, including skyrocketing unemployment, poverty, depression, and human misery.

South Africa's Curse

As in Russia, the neoliberals turned progressive change into tragedy, creating far worse conditions than under apartheid.

In 1994, the African National Congress (ANC) gained power under Mandela after generations of brutality and decades of apartheid harshness, exhibiting the worst form of racism. From 1948-1993, pass laws segregated blacks from whites and restricted their movements, requiring that pass books be carried at all times, and produced on demand under threat of arrest and prosecution. Evolving from the introduction of pass laws in 1797 until their 1986 repeal, they restricted entry to cities, forcibly relocated blacks, denied them most public services, and many forms of employment. They became apartheid's most hated symbol.

An anti-apartheid activist, Mandela was imprisoned in 1962 for life, serving 27 years until released on February 11, 1990, days after President F.W. de Klerk ended the official ban against anti-apartheid organizations, including the ANC.

Addressing the nation, Mandela said:

> I am a loyal and disciplined member of the African National Congress. I am therefore in full agreement with all of its [social justice] objectives, strategies and tactics.
>
> There must be an end to white monopoly of political power and a fundamental restructuring of our political and economic systems to ensure that the inequalities of apartheid are addressed and our society thoroughly democratized.

He quoted his own 1964 words saying he was prepared to die for "a democratic and free society in which all persons live together in harmony and with equal opportunities." As president, he reneged, surrendering totally to finance capital, though not at first rhetorically.

On May 10, 1994, two weeks after taking office, he addressed parliament, endorsing the ANC Reconstruction and Development Program (RDP) socioeconomic issues, including democracy, growth, development, reconstruction, redistribution and reconciliation. Specific concerns were housing, healthcare, land reform, jobs, education, public works, clean water, and electrification.

He called the RDP the "centerpiece of what this Government will seek to achieve, the focal point on which our attention will be continuously focused."

Five years later in his last parliamentary speech, he ignored RDP mandates after abandoning them in principle.

During his tenure, he shifted from RDP to GEAR—Growth Employment and Redistribution Program based on neoliberal free market diktats. It reflected IMF harshness, serving capital not popular needs.

State assets were privatized. Mass layoffs followed. Services were commodified, harmfully raising prices for millions. Markets were opened for trade. Taxes for corporations and the rich were cut, and social spending reduced. Bottom-line priorities trumped other issues. Record profits followed. Accessing healthcare, education and other essential services required "user fees." Few could afford them.

Wealth distribution benefitted rich whites at the expense of poor Blacks, leaving them worse off than ever, with their average income declining 19% from 1995-2000, while that of whites rose 15%.

ANC-run South Africa empowered elite Blacks, enriched white capital more than ever, and created far greater inequality, poverty and depravation than under apartheid, reflecting a neoliberal betrayal.

Free Market Repression in Haiti

Haitians enjoyed freedom briefly after their 1804 revolution transformed slaves into citizens and again during Jean-Bertrand Aristide's tenure. After US marines ousted him in February 2004, Haitian capitalism again became unfettered. The hemisphere's poorest people suffered grievously as follows:

- Thousands of public sector workers were fired.

- Many more were killed, jailed, disappeared or forced into hiding.

- Many thousands of small businesses were burned and destroyed, as well as homes for large numbers of the poor.

- Restructuring and privatizations caused unemployment and underemployment to rage with up to two-thirds of workers without reliable jobs. Haiti's rural population migrated to hard hit urban areas; work there was also scarce.

- Public sector employment was less than 1%, the lowest in the region.

- Education and health care greatly deteriorated, inadequately provided by NGOs, including church-based ones.

- Life expectancy is 53 years; death and infant mortality rates are the western hemisphere's highest.

- Haiti ranks close to lowest in sanitation systems, suffers from poor nutrition, high malnutrition, and inadequate health services and education, after positioning much higher under Aristide in these and other areas.

- It ranked poorest in the hemisphere, with 80% or more of its population lives below the poverty line; it's also the least developed with lack of infrastructure, severe deforestation and heavy soil erosion.

- Most of its population is "food insecure," and half of all children are undersized from malnutrition.

- Less than half the population has access to clean drinking water.

- The country ranks last in the hemisphere in healthcare spending with only 25 doctors and 11 nurses per 100,000 population, and most rural areas have no access to healthcare.

- Haiti has the highest HIV/AIDS incidence outside Africa.

- Haitian workers earn a below-subsistence 25 cents an hour (about $2 a day, 70 gourdes), ensuring extreme poverty and for many, too little to survive. It's less than one-fifth the 1980 minimum wage under Baby Doc Duvalier in violation of Haiti's Labor Code, Article 137, requiring annual inflation adjustments. However, corporate interests blocked changes to assure the hemisphere's lowest wage, virtual slave labor, serving as a benchmark to keep other regional labor costs from rising.

- Paramilitary UN peacekeeping (MINUSTAH) repression is severe. They were illegally sent for the first time ever to enforce a coup d'état against a democratically elected president. Political killings, kidnappings, disappearances, torture and unlawful arrests rage to prevent Haitian democracy from emerging.

Today, many months after Haiti's January 2010 earthquake, conditions on the ground are horrific. Depravation and suffering remain extreme, including raging cholera claiming thousands of lives. In November, fraudulent elections were held, excluding by far the most popular party. America colonized the country. Democracy isn't tolerated.

More than ever, Haiti is open for business, a plum to be ruthlessly exploited. Institutionalized fraud, greed, corruption and oppression are extreme. So is child trafficking and gender-based violence, including rape and other sexual abuse. Plundering Haiti's resources is planned, including its huge oil and other mineral deposits.

No wonder Washington has its fifth largest embassy in Port-au-Prince after Iraq, China, Afghanistan and Germany. Haiti is a strategic resource for its privatized sweatshops, near-slave labor, and exploitable resources, including oil, gas, gold, copper, diamonds, iridium, and zirconium, as well as valuable deep water ports. Washington wants as much of it as possible, inflicting extreme Haitian suffering to get it.

Market Fundamentalism in Afghanistan

September 11 erased the familiar world, created mass disorientation and regression, and made anything possible after the collective shock that quickly unfolded.

The "war on terror" was launched in a climate of fear. Afghanistan was first targeted. A brave new post-9/11 world was inaugurated. Its horror continues. War rages, its ferocity intense, with no end in sight after years of occupation, mass slaughter, and destruction.

War and conquest were planned well in advance, 9/11 provided the pretext to launch it. It was part of a grand strategic plan to control Central Asia's vast oil and gas reserves, then on to the grand Middle East prize in Iraq as a launching ground to exploit the entire region. Torn by endless wars and turmoil for decades, Afghans fared worst under US occupation, their ordeal unimaginable, horrific and continuing. It includes:

- Half the population is unemployed with no improvement in sight nor any planned, under market fundamentalist rules.

- Half the population earns around $200 a year with those in the booming opium trade faring marginally better.

- Poverty is soaring post-invasion, with one-fourth or more of the population needing food aid, and the regional famine risk always remaining.

- Life expectancy is one of the world's lowest at 44.5 years.

- Infant mortality is the world's highest at 161 per 1,000 births.

- One-fifth of children die before age five.

- An Afghan woman dies in childbirth every 30 minutes.

- Hundreds of thousands are homeless, forced to live in collapsed, unsafe buildings or anywhere they can.

- Less than one-fourth of the population has safe drinking water and adequate sanitation.

- Only one doctor is available per 6,000 people and one nurse per 2,500 people.

- 100 or more people are killed or wounded by unexploded ordnance monthly, and extreme violence kills many more, including regular CIA drone attacks.

- Children are kidnapped, sold into slavery or murdered for their organs, bringing high "free market" prices where everything is sold, including body parts.

- Less than 6% of Afghans have electricity, which is available only sporadically.

- Women's literacy rate is about 19%. Conditions for them are very harsh; many are forced to beg or turn to prostitution to survive.

- Schools are burned and teachers beheaded in front of students.

- Basic services don't exist and essential ones like schools, health clinics and hospitals are in deplorable condition with no aid provided to improve them as all of it goes for militarism and profiteering.

- As in Iraq, the occupying forces operate lawlessly, employing indiscriminate force, arbitrary arrests, indefinite detentions, and horrific tortures unreported in the mainstream media.

- Under military occupation, democracy is pure fantasy; the puppet president is a caricature of a leader, a willing stooge with no popular support anywhere.

- Lawlessness is rampant. War and violence rages; civilians are slaughtered daily. Dug harvesting and trafficking is uncontrolled, and corruption massive. A bitter charade of Sharia law is reinstated, and life overall is intolerable in this free market fundamentalist paradise.

Iraq: Conquered, Occupied and Plundered

Iraq has the misfortune of lying at the heart of the oil-rich Middle East where two-thirds of proven reserves are located, most of them untapped for lack of development. Its potential has remained frozen in time because of wars since 1980, economic sanctions until 2003, then conflict and occupation of the most sought after real estate on earth.

At its core, America's plan was simple—a bold new experiment to erase one nation and create another by invasion, occupation and reconstruction for pillage. It sought to transform Iraq into a privatized free market paradise, excluding benefits for its people, who are to be exploited for maximum profits.

Unfettered capitalism's record is consistent. It leaves massive human wreckage everywhere. Iraq's bold new experiment was disastrous for its people. Imperial America had other priorities in mind, including:

- controlling the region's oil, gas and other strategic resources;

- remaining permanently in the Middle East and Central Asia, besides other parts of the world; and

- achieving unchallengeable full spectrum global dominance over all land, sea, subsurface, space and information.

As a result, in the last decade alone, millions died from Washington's imperial wars, other violence, disease, depravation, torture, unimaginable human misery, and starvation. Hundreds more daily increase the numbers. Yet no one has been held accountable, despite outrageous war crimes and crimes against humanity—clear violations under international and US law. People everywhere await justice, which so far is not forthcoming.

Gideon Polya reports that according to UN data, medical literature, and other authoritative sources, the following "Iraqi Holocaust" toll from 1990-2009 is as follows:

- "1.6 million violent deaths;

- 2.8 million non-violent excess deaths;

- 1.8 million avoidable under-5 year old infant deaths;

- five to six million" internally and externally displaced persons; and

- hundreds more dying monthly.

Overall, it reflects an "Iraqi Holocaust," according to the UN Genocide Convention definition.

In addition, a climate of pervasive fear exists, as well as widespread corruption, devastation, extreme depravation, and mass impoverishment, with few basic services. There is not enough food, clean water, sanitation, electricity, health care or education. In fact, pre-Gulf War Iraq no longer exists. America effectively destroyed it, creating a noxious wasteland of vast parts of the country's territory, with the water and air contaminated by scores of pollutants, including depleted uranium (DU), chemicals, toxic metals, oil, bacteria, and other poisons.

The Tigris and Euphrates rivers are contaminated and unsafe. Imagine a cocktail of oil, gasoline, heavy metals, DU, pesticides, fertilizers, benzene, other chemicals, other pollutants, and more, poisoning water and fish, producing an epidemic of typhoid, dysentery, cholera, hepatitis, cancer, diarrhea and other diseases.

America came, conquered, occupied, and turned the Cradle of Civilization into a dystopian wasteland. Market fundamentalists like Friedman would approve. He was silent about imperial wars, lawless occupations, ruthless plunder, exploitation, vast destruction, mass detentions, rampant torture, contempt for international law, and disregard for human rights and social justice everywhere. Only unfettered markets mattered.

The Friedman Blight in America

At home, it's just as bad, short of open warfare, including:

- a democracy more fantasy than reality in a corporatist state placing profits over people;

- a burgeoning prison-industrial complex, by far the world's largest;

- social decay and growing human need;

- eroded social justice, civil liberties, human rights, and rule of law principles;

- wealth extremes at unprecedented levels;

- poverty, hunger, homelessness and unemployment the severest since the Great Depression, while corporate profits are at record highs;

- raging out-of-control militarism;

- extreme corporate and government corruption;

- a secretive, intrusive government, employing harsh police state measures against perceived enemies and open dissent;

- a de facto one party state with no checks and balances or separation of powers;

- a major media suppressing hard truths, eschewing real reporting, offering instead managed news, infotainment and junk food news; and

- better than ever times on Wall Street, the recipient of trillions of taxpayer dollars used to manipulate fraudulently for more.

That's Milton Friedman's legacy, the man *The Economist* called "the most influential economist of the second half of the 20th century (and) possibly all of it." Anointed, well funded and nurtured, he never admitted he was wrong or apologized to the millions his hokum harmed.

In fact, never have so many suffered so much as from the flimflam this ideologue preached. It reflects the dark side of "capitalism and freedom," the side Friedman's eulogies never explained and would prefer remained unknown.

Endnotes

1 Peter Coy, "Milton Friedman: Death of a Giant", *BusinessWeek*, November 17, 2006, available at <http://www.businessweek.com/bwdaily/dnflash/content/nov2006/db20061117_169299.htm>.

2 Milton Friedman, *Capitalism and Freedom*, University of Chicago Press, 1962, available at *Excerpts from Milton Friedman*, <http://www.mtholyoke.edu/acad/intrel/ipe/friedman.htm>

3 Milton Friedman, "The Biggest Ponzi Scheme on Earth", *Hoover Digest*, 1999, No. 2, April 30, 1999 < http://www.hoover.org/publications/hoover-digest/article/7523>

4 "The Caravan of Death was a Chilean Army death squad that, following the Chilean coup of 1973, flew by helicopter from south to north of Chile between September 30 and October 22, 1973. During this foray, members of the squad ordered or personally carried out the execution of at least 75 individuals held in Army custody in these garrisons. According to the NGO *Memoria y Justicia*, the squad killed 26 in the South and 71 in the North, making a total of 97 victims." "Caravan of Death", MundoAndino, <http://www.mundoandino.com/Chile/Caravan-of-Death>

GREENSPAN'S DARK LEGACY

Greenspan chaired the Federal Reserve's Board of Governors from August 11, 1987 until January 31, 2006, leaving amidst ill-deserved praise for his stewardship during good and bad times. *USA Today* noted "the onetime jazz band musician went out on a high note." The *Wall Street Journal* said "his economic legacy [rests on results] and seems secure." The *Washington Post* cited his "nearly mythical status."

Stanford Washington Research Group chief strategist Greg Valliere called him a "giant," and Bob Woodward called him "Maestro" in his cloying hagiography, published in 2000 just as Greenspan's house of cards was collapsing. The book was an adoring tribute to a man he called a symbol of American economic preeminence, whom the *Financial Times* called "An Activist Unafraid to Depart From the Rule"—by engineering massive wealth transfers from public to private hands and corporate favorites. They, of course, lauded him for services rendered.

Others also joined the chorus, praising his steady, disciplined hand on the monetary wheel, noting his success in keeping inflation and unemployment low, and representing the embodiment of prosperity, compiling a record of achievement later chairmen would be hard-pressed to match.

In 2004, William Greider, author of *Secrets of the Temple: How the Federal Reserve Runs the Country*, said otherwise, ranking Greenspan "among the most duplicitous figures to serve in modern American government." Greenspan in fact used "his exalted status as economic wizard [to] regularly corrupt the political dialogue by sowing outrageously false impressions among gullible members of Congress and adoring financial reporters."

The New York Times wrote glowingly about the man who "steer[ed] the economy through multiple calamities and ultimately....one of the longest economic booms in history....[He earned his bona fides] weather[ing] the

Black Monday stock crash of 1987 [and in 18 and a half years in office] achieved more celebrity than most rock stars." Now an author, lecturer and financial advisor, he likely matches their earnings.

His memoirs, titled *The Age of Turbulence*, reportedly got him an $8.5 million advance plus added royalties for sales exceeding 1.9 million copies. Moreover, he's in great demand on the lecture circuit at six figure fees, has his own consulting firm, Greenspan Associates LLC, and as his lawyer, Robert Barnett, earlier said, "virtually every major investment-banking firm" in the world wants to hire him for his rainmaking connections.

These have value, but not his market advice, which is best avoided. The man who engineered the largest ever stock market bubble and bust in history to that time did so through incompetence, duplicity, dereliction of duty, and subservience to the moneyed interests he represented at the expense of the kind of stable, sustained economic prosperity neither he nor Wall Street cared about.

For FIRE sector (finance, insurance and real estate) giants, he was above reproach, letting them cash in big and get plenty of advance warning when to take profits out—unlike ordinary investors who were fleeced when his house of cards collapsed.

In fact, weeks before the January 2000 market peak, he claimed "the American economy was experiencing a once-in-a-century acceleration of innovation, which propelled forward productivity, output, corporate profits and stock prices at a pace not seen in generations, if ever."

It was hokum on a par with famed economist/professor Irving Fisher's remarks before the 1929 stock market crash and Great Depression, quoted in Chapter 1. Fisher kept insisting that recovery was just around the corner, the way Wall Street touts it today, preying on gullible investors, who are mindless of how easily they're scammed. No matter how many previous times they have been taken, they're always easy prey. As a result, fraudsters take full advantage, especially financial giants, who are experts at doing it.

Wall Street's "Maestro," aided them, saying at the height of the internet bubble:

> Lofty equity prices have reduced the cost of capital. The result has been a veritable explosion of spending on high-tech equipment... And I see nothing to suggest that these opportunities will peter out anytime soon... Indeed many argue that the pace of innovation will continue to quicken... to exploit the still largely untapped potential for e-commerce, especially the business-to-business arena.

A week later, the Nasdaq peaked at 5048, then crashed to a low of 1114 on October 9, 2002, losing 78% of its value. The S&P 500 dropped 49%, with retail investors losing out while Greenspan engineered more bubbles with a tsunami of easy money. It got respected investor Jeremy Grantham to compare his handiwork to a giant suspension bridge, saying in 2007:

> Thousands of bolts hold it together. Today a few of them have fractures and one or two seem to have failed completely. The bridge, however, with typical redundancy built in can [easily take a few failed bolts], perhaps quite a few....The global financial structure is far too large and has far too many interlocking pieces for weakening US house prices and a few subprime issues to bring it down.

What worried him was "broad-based financial metal fatigue," causing simultaneous failures "with ultimately disastrous consequences." Months later that occurred. The market recovered two years later, but it remains fragile, and has left growing Main Street millions unemployed, underemployed, underpaid, losing benefits, and unaided by federal and local governments when they most need help, a topic addressed later in the book.

Greenspan's Background and Tenure as Federal Reserve Chairman

Raised in New York, Greenspan got his BA and MA in economics at New York University, then a PhD in economics from Columbia without completing the dissertation a degree usually requires. In a highly unusual move, Columbia exempted him.Early on, he became enamored with free market ideologue Ayn Rand (1905-1982), wrote for her newsletters and authored three essays for her book titled, *Capitalism: The Unknown Ideal*. It expressed her views on the system's "moral aspects," including her attempt (with Greenspan's help) to rescue it from its "alleged champions who are responsible for the fact that capitalism is being destroyed without a hearing [or] trial, without any public knowledge of its principles, its nature, its history, or its moral meaning."

That was 1966, when Rand, a staunch libertarian like Greenspan, believed fundamentalist capitalism was being battered by a flood of altruism in the wake of New Deal and Great Society programs she (and Greenspan) deplored. She defended big business and imperial lawlessness, at the same time denouncing rebellious students and altruism's evils. Greenspan concurred, was associated with her for 20 years, and never looked back. From 1948 until his 1987 Federal Reserve appointment, he was:

- Richard Nixon's 1968 campaign domestic policy coordinator;

- Gerald Ford's Council of Economic Advisers Chairman; and

- from 1955-1987, head of Townsend-Greenspan & Company economic consultants. In fact, its forecasting record was so poor, it faced liquidation when he left to join the Fed.

A former competitor, Pierre Renfret, remarked:

> When Greenspan closed down his economic consulting business to go on the Board of the Federal Reserve, he did so because he had no clients left, and the business was going under. We even went so far as to try and hire some of his former employees only to find out he had none for the 6 months prior to his closing. When he closed down he did not have a single client left on a retainer basis.[1]

That made him Reagan's perfect Fed Chairman choice, Renfret added. It was Greenspan's failure in private business that got him into government service in the first place, letting him betray working Americans like he failed clients.

He didn't disappoint. As Wall Street's front man, he bailed it out in 1987 after the disastrous October Black Monday. In 1998, he did it again, helping Long Term Capital Management escape collapse. Then an encore in 2000 after the dot-com bubble burst.

His favorite monetary medicine worked fine short-term when used as directed—floods of easy money followed by more. He was oblivious to the fact that the cure was worse than the disease, a lesson his successor never learned either, engineering an even greater house of cards than the "maestro," a topic later addressed.

In his memoirs, Greenspan claimed otherwise, producing a breathtaking example of historical revisionism. No wonder author Peter Hartcher called him "Bubble Man" in his book by that title.[2] He quoted Bob Woodward saying Greenspan "believed he had done all he could" to contain over-exuberance when, in fact, he engineered it:

1. Greenspan argued that he didn't support George Bush's regressive tax cuts for the rich (that helped create huge budget deficits). In fact, he did, and in 2001 wholeheartedly endorsed Bush's centerpiece economic policy in testimony before the Senate Budget Committee. At the time, he cited the economic slowdown saying: "Should current economic weakness spread.... having a tax cut [to the rich, of course]...may...do noticeable good."

2. He also admitted what's politically inconvenient to acknowledge:

that "the Iraq war is largely about oil," yet later claimed he wasn't "saying that that's the administration's motive. I'm just saying that if somebody asked me, are we fortunate in taking out Saddam? I would say it was essential." He failed to acknowledge his Bush agenda support across the board, including for the Afghan and Iraq wars, giving earlier reasons he later retracted. Throughout his career and thereafter, he notoriously tried having it both ways, saying one thing, then practicing another.

3. He took no responsibility for the 2000 dot-com bubble, falsely claiming he never saw it coming while fueling it generously with liquidity. In December 1996, after acknowledging the market's "irrational exuberance," he failed to curb it by raising interest rates, margin requirements, and jawboning investors to cool overheated market conditions to restore stability for long-term sustainable growth. Instead, he filled the punch bowl rather than removing it, created a bubble, and let it burst, causing irreparable harm to millions of small investors and working households, still reeling from his policies and his successor's—both loyal servants of power.

4. He claimed no responsibility for the housing and bond bubbles he created by cutting interest rates aggressively to 1%, then flooding the markets with liquidity. As things got out of hand, timely action could have avoided the 2007 credit crisis. Again, he made a bad situation worse, kept the party going, and let Wall Street profit hugely at the public's expense. Despite an unprecedented $8 trillion housing bubble, he derided critics saying anything was wrong. He even recommended homebuyers take out subprime and adjustable rate mortgages, the very practice that created America's greatest real estate crisis which even now is still unwinding. But Alan Greenspan isn't around to answer for gross malfeasance, causing millions to lose their most valuable asset and jobs in a weak economy.

5. He avoided responsibility for letting outstanding debt more than triple on his watch, a record his successor exceeded, placing an enormous burden on future generations, too great, in fact, to bear.

Greenspan's Role in the Greatest Ever Wealth Transfer from Public to Private Hands—Exceeded Only by His Successor Who Continues It to This Day

Greenspan was a one-man wrecking crew years before becoming Fed Chairman. Moreover, his early role assured power elites he was safe, a man to rely on. In fact, he earned his stripes and then some in charge of the National Commission on Social Security Reform (called the Greenspan Commission).[3]

Appointed by Ronald Reagan in 1981, he chaired it to study and recommend actions to deal with "the short-term financing crisis that Social Security faced....[claiming that the] Old-Age, Survivors and Disability Insurance Trust Fund (OASDI) would run out of money....as early as August, 1983."

It was a hoax no different from today's false claims, but major media reports never explained that, nor do they now. In fact, they supported the Commission's transfer of trillions of public dollars into private hands. As a result, to that time, it was the greatest heist ever attempted, in plain sight, with variations on the claims still ongoing, yet no one cries foul to stop it.

In January 1983, the Commission's report was issued. Congress then used it to enact 1983 Social Security Amendments to "resolve short-term financing problem[s]and [make] many other significant changes in Social Security law." In fact, people were none the wiser, unaware they'd been scammed.

While the Commission recommended that:

- Social Security remain government funded, not a voluntary program for that would destroy it;

- $150 - 200 billion in either additional income or decreased outgo be provided the OASDI (Old Age, Survivors, and Disability Insurance) in calendar years 1983-89;

- the actuarial imbalance for the 75 year Trust Funds valuation period of an average 1.80% of taxable payroll be resolved;

it also recommended:

- a "consensus package" to fix the problem by raising payroll taxes on incomes, but exempting the rich beyond a maximum level taxed

- gradually increasing the retirement age and various other suggested short and longer range options.

The result was that low income earners today pay more payroll than income tax, and bottom level ones are especially burdened. They pay no income tax, but aren't exempt from 6.2% of earnings for Social Security and another 1.45% for Medicare, up to a maximum $106,800, matched by employers.

In 2011, the Social Security payroll tax is 4.2%, a one year drop to be possibly extended or made permanent. Another chapter discusses the implications. As of January 1, 1984, it was ruled that:

- Mandatory OASDI coverage be extended to all newly hired federal government and NGO civilian employees.

- State and local governments electing employee OASDI-HI coverage be prevented from terminating it in future years.

But it was also ruled that:

- The method of computing benefits be revised to exclude accruable benefits to individuals from non-covered OASDI employment, and only apply to their period of eligibility—to eliminate "windfall" benefits.

- 50% of OASDI benefits henceforth be taxable as ordinary income for individuals earning $20,000 or more and married couples $25,000 or more. (In 1993, 85% was taxable for higher-income retirees.)

- More is taxable as well, including cost of living adjustments, survivor's benefits for spouses who remarry after age 60, divorced spouses, disabled widows and widowers, as well as scheduled payroll tax increases to cease after 1990. (In fact, the taxable base increased from $97,500 in 2007 to $106,800 currently.)

- In addition, beginning in 1984, self-employed persons pay the combined 12.4% employer-employee rate, half considered a business expense, along with other changes that benefit high income earners at the expense of lower and middle income ones— the scam's idea in the first place.

Yet in 1983, people had been told the proposed changes would make Social Security fiscally sound for the next 75 years. However, no problem existed in the first place. In fact, Greenspan's mandate was to transfer massive public wealth to private hands.

It was just one part of an overall Reagan administration scheme that included huge individual and corporate tax cuts from 1981 to 1986. The rich benefitted most with top rates dropping from 70% in 1981 to 50% over three years, then to 28% in 1986 while the bottom rate actually rose from 11 to 15%.

It was the first time US income tax rates were ever reduced at the top and raised at the bottom simultaneously. But it was far worse than that. In only a few years, Reagan enacted the largest ever US income tax cut (mostly for the rich) while instituting the greatest ever increase entirely against working Americans earning $30,000 or less.

Alan Greenspan engineered it by supporting income tax cuts while doubling the payroll tax to defray the revenue shortfall. He also recommended raiding the Social Security Trust Fund to offset deficits, and who'd know the difference? His scheme helped make the US tax code hugely regressive as well as transform a pay-as-you-go retirement/disability program to a wage earner-subsidized one for the rich besides supporting current beneficiaries. It was a cleverly conceived scam, Greenspan promoting it as a rescue package for ordinary earners. It was nothing of the sort—then or today.

As a consequence, the wealth gap widened, continued under Clinton, became unprecedented under George W. Bush, and more extreme than ever under Obama, who was elected primarily to serve Wall Street. Like Bush and his predecessors, he supports tax cuts for the rich, enormous public wealth transfers to America's aristocracy, and outrageous corporate subsidies, leaving low and middle income earners stuck with out-of-control deficits, deep social service cuts, mindless militarism, a $1.5 trillion war budget, and Wall Street licensed to loot the federal treasury with impunity.

Yet we're told that Social Security and Medicare:

- are going broke;

- need essential "reforms;"

- that delaying them punishes younger workers and threatens both programs with insolvency; and

- that cutting benefits is essential to saving the programs, including raising the retirement age, means testing the system, privatizing it, and/or making working Americans pay more but get less. A later chapter addresses the issue in detail.

A Final Comment

A generation of financial manipulation has devastated working Americans, but it's much worse than that. The trends, instruments and policies include:

- the financialization of the American and Western economies, giving privatized money control unbridled power;

- destructive neoliberal globalization, a malignancy ravaging world economies;

- corrupted IMF and World Bank policies;

- America's permanent war strategy;

- automation killing jobs;

- offshoring millions of jobs to low wage countries;

- permanently losing many other jobs;

- shifting from high-wage/good benefits manufacturing jobs to low-wage/weak or no benefits services ones;

- part-time jobs replacing higher-paying full-time ones;

- eroding social benefits with a view to ending them entirely;

- deregulation, creating a license to steal with impunity;

- targeting organized labor for destruction;

- mass privatizations, including public education, water, public lands, buildings and roads, state parks, airports, prisons, and other properties to raise cash; and

- leaving Washington more than ever corporate occupied territory, especially dominated by FIRE sector giants and militarists, including all war-profiteering companies.

Ronald Reagan began a generational wealth transfer well exceeding $1 trillion annually through 2007. From then until now, Wall Street alone minimally got $12.4 trillion and likely much more, besides hundreds of billions more shifted from public to private hands—a scam exceeding the worst of Alan Greenspan's fleecing as Fed chairman and head of Reagan's Social Security Commission.

Between Greenspan, Bernanke, and corrupted Bush and Obama administration officials, the federal treasury was massively looted for the rich, with the public none the wiser about decades of outrageous scams. They're ongoing because Republicans and Democrats endorse them, flouting the rule of law and democratic values which they only scorn and reject, heading America for tyranny and ruin.

Endnotes

1   Dave Lindorf, "Greenspan's Pension", *Counterpunch*, March 4, 2004, available at <http://www.counterpunch.com/lindorff03042004.html>

2   Peter Hartcher, *Bubble Man: Alan Greenspan and the Missing 7 Trillion Dollars*, W. W. Norton, New York, 2006.

3   Available at <http://www.ssa.gov/history/reports/gspan.html>

4

A SHORT HISTORY OF US GOVERNMENT HANDOUTS

Crisis bailouts and handouts to banks and other corporate favorites aren't a new phenomenon in America. Not at all, a topic Howard Zinn addressed in an October 2008 *Guardian* article titled, "From Empire to Democracy," saying:

> Let's face a historical truth: we have never had a "free market," we have always had government intervention in the economy, and indeed that intervention has been welcomed by the captains of finance and industry. They had no quarrel with 'big government' when it served their needs.[1]

It started way back in 1787 when the Constitution was drafted. The year before, farmers from Western Massachusetts and elsewhere rebelled to protect their properties from being seized for nonpayment of taxes. The Founders took note and "created 'big government' powerful enough" to deter future incidents, return runaway slaves to their owners, and massacre Indians to make land available for new settlers and wealthy property owners.

Early on, the idea of handouts was established, at first to pay full value for near-worthless bonds held by speculators. It was an earlier version of buying today's toxic assets at near-full value or trading them for US Treasuries—essentially swapping good money for bad, a deal only financial giants get.

That was bad enough, then it was compounded by taxing the public to pay for it each time, and having a standing army ready in case of resistance. That's precisely what happened in 1794 when Pennsylvania farmers rebelled against unfair tax laws.

"In the first sessions of the first Congress," markets were manipulated with tariffs to subsidize manufacturers. Government also partnered with private banks to establish a national market. These practices were commonplace from then until now. Only the amounts got bigger, with the stakes today far higher.

The more concentrated business gets, the greater its appetite and the more power it has to satisfy it. Now it's insatiable enough to demand trillions in handouts as well as license to loot the federal Treasury—with taxpayers getting the bill.

In the 19th century, Zinn said, government subsidized the building of canals, the merchant marine and, before and during the Civil War, gave about 100 million free acres of land to railroad barons "along with considerable loans to keep" them in business. It was the largest ever giveaway until Treasury Secretary Paulson's-engineered Wall Street one, followed by Geithner's, far exceeding that. It was just the beginning and has never stopped, much of it secret and unreported.

Democrats, in fact, back support for business more than do Republicans. This is another long-standing tradition since the republic's inception, as Zinn observed. But when state support is requested for the needy, it's a non-starter. Democrat Grover Cleveland vetoed

> a bill to give [a mere] $100,000 to Texas farmers to help them buy seed grain during a drought, saying [dismissively]: 'Federal aid in such cases encourages the expectation of paternal care on the part of the government and weakens the sturdiness of our national character.' [2]

However, in the same year, he gave wealthy bondholders $5 million by pricing them $28 above market value. "Rugged individualism" he called it to make it on our own with little government intervention for assistance—that's only for big business, of course, never the public. There is no history of American governments undertaking development projects with an eye to the priorities, best interests and well being of the American people, which is the whole point of having an elected, democratic government. The role of a democratic government is to decide what's needed by the public, not just to accede to corporate wishes and build what suits them. Development should serve everyone, not special interests.

After WW II, Keynesianism became dogma, but it was *military* Keynesianism. Aircraft and other defense industries had to be saved to avoid another Depression, it was claimed. The oil industry got its depletion allowance. Chrysler was resurrected from the dead. Continental Illinois Bank was taken over until sold to Bank of America. Business was shored up overall by the 1971 Emergency Loan Guarantee Act.

Post-9/11, the Air Transportation Safety and Stabilization Act was passed to help airlines. Current help has rescued Wall Street, Fannie,

Freddie, AIG, the auto giants, select corporate favorites, and others called "too big to fail."

Historian Charles Beard's Documented History of Handouts

In December 1931, noted historian Charles Beard wrote about earlier instances of handouts to big business for *Harper's Monthly* in an article titled: "The Myth of Rugged American Individualism."[3] He documented 15 examples of government handouts/subsidies to business when the country was sinking into Depression. It demolished the notion that business had single-handedly achieved the building of the country (or even its own special projects) due to the acumen and strength of character of big American entrepreneurs, revealing the extent to which government (as funded by the taxpayer) was not just instrumental, but an indispensable participant. That might have been alright where public and business interests coincided, such as in the provision of general infrastructure—but more frequently government was engaged in these projects in such a way that corporations were the primary beneficiaries to the detriment of the public—such as the elaborate construction of networks of highways favoring the auto industry and Big Oil instead of cheap public transit.

The giant businesses have enjoyed tremendous benefits while commanding the public policy agenda, distorting public policy priorities and expenditures in ways that are not in (or are even against) the public interest. And then, even as they reap immense government subsidies, they have had the face to preach "individualism" and self-sufficiency to the American public, to tell Americans that we should demand nothing/expect nothing from the government we elected to address our needs.

1. *Government Regulation of Railways from 1887*

Beard asked: "How did the Government get into this business?" At the "insistence of business men, shippers, who were harassed and sometimes ruined by railway tactics." It was through rebates, pools, stock watering, bankruptcy-juggling, savage rate slashing, merciless competition, and much more by some of the most cut-throat of all robber barons.

Disastrous railway bankruptcies, involving bloodshed and arson during the Panic of 1873, resulted from financier Jim Fisk and railroad baron Jay Gould trying to corner the gold market. Ulysses S. Grant deterred them. A panic ensued and depression followed—two years after the great Chicago fire destroyed four square city miles.

2. *Waterways*

Since the nation's founding, government spent hundreds of millions of dollars funding the development of rivers, harbors, canals, and other infrastructure, and continues doing it for business. "Who (was) back of all this," Beard asked? "Business men and farmers who want lower freight rates. There is not a chamber of commerce on any Buck Creek in America that will not cheer until tonsils are cracked for any proposal to make the said creek navigable." Dredging companies also backed it and companies making their machinery.

3. *The United States Barge Corporation*

Again Beard asked: "Who got the Government into the job of running barges on some of its improved waterways?" Not socialists. Good Republicans and Democrats representing the country's business interests.

4. *The Shipping Business*

WW I was the proximate cause. For over half a century, government stayed out of subsidizing ship builders and allied industries. "Under the cover of war necessities," it went into the business with much joy from the industry. It backed huge merchant marine expenditures in the form of cheap or subsidized funding, and did it by spending money "like water educating politicians." Today we call it lobbying.

Beard asked: "Who wants navy officers on half pay to serve on privately owned ships? Business men. Who wants the Government to keep on operating ships on 'pioneer' lines that do not pay? Business men. And when the United States Senate gets around to investigating this branch of business, it will find more entertainment than the Trade Commission has found in the utility inquest."

5. *Aviation*

Government was already in this business by providing costly airway services free of charge and by subsidizing air mail. Once again, private enterprise was behind the whole scheme, or as Beard put it: "Gentlemen engaged in aviation and the manufacture of planes and dirigibles." Government merely helped out by buying planes "for national defense" or whatever other reason it chose.

6. *Canals*

Consider the Panama Canal, for example. East and West coast shippers backed it because of costly railroad rates. Others with a financial interest in the Cape Cod Canal found that one unprofitable. "They rejoiced to see [that] burden placed on the broad back of our dear Uncle Sam" to bail them out.

7. *Highway Building*

Even in Beard's day, "business men engaged in the manufacture and sale of automobiles and trucks" wanted the government to spend hundreds of millions on roads and tax railroads to help pay for them. With a touch of humor, Beard asked: "Who proposes to cut off every cent of that outlay? Echoes do not answer." Beyond Beard's timeline, the Eisenhower administration built much of the Interstate Highway System at the behest of the auto industry, but its origin way pre-dated him with the Federal-Aid Highway Act of 1938. Then another Federal-Aid Highway Act of 1944. Still another in 1952, and under Eisenhower one more plus the Highway Revenue Act of 1956 that created the Highway Trust Fund to pay for the proposed 41,000 miles of roads (up to almost 47,000 by 2004).

8. *The Department of Commerce*

Its very name defines its purpose—to promote what Calvin Coolidge called "the business of America," a process Beard described as going on in its "magnificent mansion near the Treasury Department, and its army of hustlers scouting for business at the uttermost ends of the earth. Who is responsible for loading on the Government the job of big drummer at large for business? Why shouldn't these rugged individualists do their own drumming instead of asking taxpayers to do it for them?"

Herbert Hoover headed the department at the time and outdid all his predecessors in dispensing public money. The same president Hoover deserves blame for his public stinginess after the country headed into Depression on his watch.

9. *The Big Pork Barrel*

It's been around for ages and entered into the vocabulary after the Civil War. It was named after a container to store pig meat in brine, and in 1801 a farmer's almanac urged readers to "mind our pork and cider barrels." Its need went out with refrigeration but got new life in reference to political bills bringing home the bacon for constituents, building all sorts of things like post offices, rivers, harbors, buildings, and a whole array of boondoggle projects and giveaways. Beard cited public buildings, navy yards and army posts with business interests every time the beneficiaries rather than public need.

10. *The Bureau of Standards (NBS)*

It's now called the National Institute for Standards and Technology (NIST), and was originally established in 1901 as a measurement standards lab under the Department of Commerce to promote US innovation and industrial competitiveness. Given its purpose was to help business, Beard asked: "Why shouldn't they do their own [promoting] at their own expense, instead of turning to the Government?" Why indeed, but they do at taxpayer expense!

11. *The Federal Trade Commission*

In 1914, it was established as an independent US government agency. While claiming its principal mission is to promote "consumer protection," it exists solely for business, and in Beard's day for "business men who do not like to be outwitted or cheated by their competitors." Why so for "rugged individualists," he asked? Why not let them all do as they please "without invoking government intervention at public expense" withno public benefit.

12. *The Anti-trust Acts*

Beard referred to the 1890 Sherman Antitrust Act and 1914 Clayton Antitrust Act—trustbusting legislation of their day to defuse anti-competititive practices. Today they're mere artifacts at a time when business oligopolies and monopolies dominate all major industries and are practically omnipotent. It's why Chomsky calls them "private tryannies," the most tyrannical and omnipotent on Wall Street.

Earlier, businesses complained that these laws constrained their ability to do large-scale planning without risking prosecution. Yet farmers and small businesses wanted them. The former for lower prices. The latter so as not to be undersold, "beaten by clever tricks, or crushed to the wall by competitors with immense capital."

The rugged individualism of *small* businesspeople inspired both acts, what Woodrow Wilson called "the New Freedom. Break up the trusts," he said, "and let each tub stand on its own bottom." That's how small businessmen felt. Lawyers representing them put it differently: "The natural person's personal liberty should not be destroyed by artificial persons known as corporations created under the auspices of the State."

13. *The Tariff*

The imposition of tariffs goes back to the 18th century; they were the government's largest source of revenue from the 1790s until WW I. Once income taxes became law in 1913, that changed, although taxing income was used during the Civil War and again in the 1890s.

Beard referred to tariffs as the kind of "interference" business men demanded to protect their interests while, at the same time, wanting "the right of capital to find its most lucrative course, industry and intelligence their natural reward, and commodities their fair price."

The idea of "free trade" then was about the way it is now—one way, with government protecting business against foreign competition, heavily by tariffs back then, while seeking to gain free access to the markets of other states—demonstrated more today by the WTO, NAFTA. CAFTA-DR, and other destructive trade deals. Beard's earlier response: "If competition is good, why not stand up and take it?"

14. *The Federal Farm Board*

It was created in 1929 so it was quite new when Beard wrote about it. He called it a "collectivist institution," a product of "agrarian agitation on the part of our most stalwart individualists, the free and independent farmers."

Hoover sponsored it and signed it into law, but under him its measures were modest at best. It primarily and fundamentally stabilized prices and production through cooperative methods. It financed associations to limit production. The alternative was to let farmers produce what they wish, as much as they could, and sell it at whatever the market would bear. Its slogan was "Grow Less—Get More," cooperate under government leadership or hang separately.

15. *The Moratorium and Frozen Assets*

It was Herbert Hoover's plan for a one-year moratorium on payments due the US from foreign powers at a time of growing economic duress, as well as a "proposal to give public support to 'frozen assets.' " Its "inspiration" was the jam American investment bankers were in. They made easy money in the 1920s, were then in trouble, and wanted government bailout help.

In 1927, a distinguished German economist told Beard that "the great game in his country, as in other parts of Europe, was to borrow billions from private bankers in the US, so that it would ultimately be impossible to pay reparations, the debts due the Federal Government, and then the debts owed to private parties." As a result, they believed bankers would force their government to forego its claims for the benefit of private operators. It worked, and according to Beard: "American taxpayers [were] to be soaked and American bankers [were] to collect— perhaps."

What then is a "frozen asset?" A piece of paper representing a transaction expecting to yield a larger return than possible on a prudent investment. For example, a 7% Western farm mortgage at the time was frozen tight and its holder with it. But why should government have to intervene to save them from "their folly and greed? No reason, except that [investors] want the Government to bring home their cake so they can eat it."

Beard stressed that "the Federal government does not operate in a vacuum, but under impulsion from without." From "rugged individualists—

business men or farmers or both....The Government operates continually in the midst of the most powerful assembly of lobbyists the world has ever seen." They represent every business interest "above the level of a corner grocery. For forty years or more there has not been a President, Republican or Democrat, who has not talked against government interference and then supported measures adding more interference to the huge collection already accumulated."

Woodrow Wilson, for example, based his 1912 campaign on individualism, new freedom against corporate wealth controlling government, he called it. As a Jeffersonianism heir, "he decried paternalism of every kind." But look at the laws enacted under him:

- the Federal Reserve Act, subverting the Constitution by giving banking giants the right to print money, control its supply and price, and charge government interest on what it would not have to pay if it created its own;

- the Federal income tax to service the federal debt owed to bankers;

- the trainmen's law, virtually fixing wages on interstate railways for certain classes of employees;

- the shipping board law that put the government in the shipping business and let it regulate rates;

- the Farm Loan Act, establishing 12 regional Farm Loan Banks to serve members of Farm Loan Associations;

- federal aid for highway construction;

- the Alaskan railway;

- the Water Power Act, creating a Federal Power Commission with extensive authority over waterways and the construction and use of water power projects; and

- various other acts belying the notion of "the less government the better," for helping business became the law of the land.

Republicans regained power in the early 1920s on a slogan of returning to normalcy and getting the government out of business. In fact, they repealed none of Wilson's laws. They and their ideological forebears "came honestly by subsidies, bounties, internal improvements, tariffs, and other aids to business." It was their kind of normalcy. Individualism, with no interference, lots of handouts, and nothing has changed under Republican and Democrat administrations through to today.

Handouts to Business: the American Way of Life

Socialized costs and privatized profits define American business—more than ever today with multi-trillions in handouts plus all sorts of other generous benefits, including:

- subsidies and other direct grants;

- tax breaks, reductions, deductions, exclusions, write-offs, exemptions, credits, loopholes, shelters, and rebates even for profitable companies; the bigger they are, the more they get;

- letting corporations be headquartered offshore and pay no federal income taxes; allowing them to repatriate foreign earnings on the same basis, export jobs and erode the nation's industrial base, financialize the economy, practice casino capitalism, and loot the Treasury to cover bad debts from speculation and shoddy/corrupted business practices;

- issuing large government contracts of every imaginable kind; some no-bid, others on a cost-plus basis with every incentive to cheat and get more;

- providing discounted user fees or subsidized use of public resources;

- free government-funded R & D;

- various other government direct payments, with every cabinet department a conduit for government funding to private business; every program from the Department of Commerce, Agriculture and others to underwrite it—the FDA for Big Pharma; the FCC for media and telecommunications firms; the FAA for the airlines, the Treasury, Fed, and SEC for Wall Street, and so forth; the IRS and FBI are the most active "peoples" agencies, ignoring mega-crooks to focus on minor ones;

- other subsidies like accelerated depreciation; aid for the cost of advertising, with direct aid for companies that advertise abroad; and much more with Democrats as pro-business as Republicans while at the same time curtailing essential social benefits;

- individual tax breaks for the rich; winking and nodding about trillions offshored to tax havens; letting corporate fraud and abuse become the national pastime;

- privatizing more of what government should do and/or does best, including schools, highways, bridges, airports, prisons, public lands, and utilities; privatizing research and the exploration of outer space, the running of elections, and the military; expanding their wars through the use of mercenaries, and setting their sights on taking away the most important poverty reduction program for seniors and the disabled—Social Security; plus another to end Medicare and Medicaid;

- privatizing wealth and socializing debt;

- abolishing welfare and other social benefits; rendering organized labor impotent in a "Walmartized" society; ruling by the doctrine of rewarding the privileged at the expense of real democracy, beneficial social change, the greater good, government for the people and their needs, and the notion that government should serve everyone equitably, not just a privileged few.

Beard's "rugged individualism" is pure myth and self-congratulation. But rugged or otherwise, "individualism" is the consigned fate for the rest of us—who are left to sink or swim at a time when millions have been submerged, with millions more joining them in a nation that long ago betrayed its own, serving wealth and power interests alone.

Endnotes

1   Howard Zinn, "From empire to democracy," *The Guardian*, October 2, 2008. Available at <http://www.guardian.co.uk/commentisfree/2008/oct/02/usa.creditcrunch>
2   Howard Zinn, *A People's History of the United States,* Harper & Row, p. 253.
3   Available at <http://www.harpers.org/archive/1931/12/0018146>

5

QUANTITATIVE EASING:

ELIXIR OR POISON?

Ahead of the November 2010 G-20 meeting in Seoul, South Korea, the Fed announced its second foray into quantitative easing—QE II—pumping another $600 billion into the economy between then and end of June 2011. It would be a flexible figure to be raised or lowered freely, with the Fed saying it would:

> ...regularly review the pace of its securities purchases and the overall size of the asset-purchase program in light of incoming information and will adjust the program as needed to best foster maximum employment and price stability.

An additional $300 billion received from maturing securities will also be used. Easing, in fact, began around mid-year. Wall Street insiders knew about it and could take advantage, but not the public. Effectively, QE debauches the currency, harms the economy, and destroys, not creates, jobs. It lets the favored recipients offshore it to BRIC countries (Brazil, Russia, India, China) and tax havens.

Market Ticker's Karl Denninger called QE "the largest tax ever imposed on the American people in the history of the nation. It is more than fourteen times the Bush tax cuts...Goldman Sachs believes that Bernanke will impose a total tax through [QE] of more than four trillion dollars over the next two years, or more than fifty-seven times the Bush tax cuts."[1]

How so? Because the credit created is going into asset markets (stocks, bonds, commodities, etc. which are largely offshore), not into the economy. QE I's tax, in fact, diluted stimulus funds; it was effectively an offsetting tax going "directly into the bankers' pockets" for speculation, big salaries and bonuses.

Add to that potential inflation later on. According to James Grant of *Grant's Interest Rate Observer*, QE will create unsustainable asset bubbles and debase the dollar, making products and services more expensive, ending "everyday low prices."[2] Bernanke wants inflation, a hidden tax. Devaluation is being used to get it, no matter the serious consequences.

In his 1920 book, *The Economic Consequences of the Peace*, John Maynard Keynes warned:

> Lenin...was certainly right. There is no subtler, no surer means of overturning the existing basis of society than to debauch the currency. The process engages all the hidden forces of economic law on the side of destruction, and does it in a manner which not one man in a million is able to diagnose.

Denninger was just as blunt, saying unless public outrage stops this:

> you're all going to be effectively dead economically.
> Your assets will be stripped.
> All of them.
> Your homes.
> Your businesses.
> Your savings...And, when the inevitable margin collapse comes in the corporate sector, your stock portfolio will detonate again and your pension funds, Medicare, Medicaid and Social Security will be [toast].[3]

There's no middle ground, no place to hide. Either "stop this madness or we all get destroyed. Those are the only choices," or as Tom Lehrer's memorable 1950s lyrics put it, referring then to potential nuclear annihilation, "we'll all go together when we go." All except Wall Street, of course, which is profiting all the way to the "bank."

On November 4, 2010 on Bloomberg TV, David Stockman, Reagan's Office of Management and Budget Director, explained it this way: Fed QE "is injecting high grade monetary heroin into the financial system of the world, and one of these days it is going to kill the patient,"[4] meaning economies and people.

In early 2009, economist Michael Hudson said:

> The [US] economy has reached its debt limit and is entering its insolvency phase. We are not in a cycle but [at] the end of an era. The old world of debt pyramiding to a fraudulent degree cannot be restored[5]

only delayed to postpone a painful day of reckoning.

Piling new debt on old exacerbates a bad situation. Hudson explained more in his 2010 article titled, "US 'Quantitative Easing' is Fracturing the Global Economy."[6]

Quantitative Easing (QE) Defined

In simple terms, QE is monetary policy to increase the money supply—literally creating it out of thin air. Wikipedia calls it central bank policy "to increase the supply of money by increasing excess reserves of the banking system. This policy is usually invoked when the normal methods to control the money supply have failed." Or have been exhausted in cases where interest rates are near zero, today's situation in America, Japan and elsewhere.

Central banks do it electronically, thereby increasing their own accounts to use any way they wish, but not risk free. Though not evident so far, too much money chasing too few goods causes inflation. Currency debasing, including forcing down the dollar, is another issue, very relevant today, given that it's part of the Fed's plan. Gold prices reflect it, nearly quintupling from under $300 in 2002. Experts, in fact, believe it's heading much higher. Bond rates so far are low, reflecting economic weakness, but once inflation is sensed, they'll rise proportionately to the risk.

Project Censored's top 2009-10 story is the plan to replace the dollar, perhaps by debasing it to worthlessness. However, other nations have reacted, Michael Hudson says, by "creat[ing] an international monetary system in which central bank savings do not fund [America's massive debt]. Russia, China, India and Brazil have taken the lead."

Others will likely follow. "Finance has become the new mode of warfare." Currency wars are in play for economic competitiveness, with nations jockeying with each other during a period of economic weakness—a game putting them all at risk.

QE "is based on the wrong-headed idea that if the Fed provides liquidity, banks will...lend out credit at a markup, 'earning their way out of debt'—inflating the economy in the process."

Not the economy most people think of, however. The Fed's targeting "asset markets—above all real estate, as 80% of [US] bank loans"[7] are for mortgages.

Importantly, Fed gamesmanship puts international finance at risk. "This is what US economic policy and even its foreign policy is now all about, including de-criminalizing financial fraud." In the 1980s, "greed was good," including massive fraud, but that is way exceeded now. Today, in fact, it reaches levels never before imagined in unknown multi-trillions, with lots more to come unless stopped.

Instead of healing ailing economies, the Fed is wrecking them. Hoped for new borrowing isn't happening. Instead, banks tightened their loan standards rather than lend more to US homeowners, consumers and businesses.

Instead of banks lending domestically, dollars are being flooded into world currency markets, in the hope that insolvent banks can earn their way out of debt, and make America more competitive by debasing the dollar, perhaps replacing it.

Domestically, the market is "loaned up." Borrowing is shrinking, not expanding, a sure way to prevent economic growth. QE I—the $1.7 trillion created from March 2009 to March 2010—failed. More worrisome, according to Hudson, is that QE II entails

> consequences that Federal Reserve policy makers have not acknowledged. For one thing, the banks have used [bailout and liquidity funds] to increase their profits and to continue paying high salaries and bonuses. What their lending is inflating are asset prices, [not output and employment]. And asset price inflation is increasing the power of property over living labor and production, elevating the FIRE sector (finance, insurance, and real estate) further over the 'real' economy.

Moreover, QE II is a zero sum game. It can only work at the expense of other economies. That's why it's "financial aggression," destroying global currency stability. It also harms America, with the greater economy being sacrificed for the FIRE sector, especially Wall Street, while destroying countries and human beings for profit.

Today's "global economy is being turned into a tributary system, achieving what military conquest sought in times past." It's implicit in QE II. However, other countries are reacting, "taking defensive measures against this speculation [and] 'free credit' takeovers" with cheap dollars, using various methods to do it.

The Reserve Bank of India raised interest rates multiple times. So did the Reserve Bank of Australia, as did China to cool its overheated economy and monstrous housing bubble, far larger than America's at its peak, a likely accident waiting to happen. Brazil raised its tax on foreign investment in government bonds. South Korea reinstated a withholding tax on interest payable to foreign investors in government bonds. Other nations are considering similar measures, mindful of Fed policy.

According to Hudson, the "major international economic question... is how national economies can achieve greater stability by insulating themselves from predatory [Fed] financial movements," a zero sum game they'll lose if they can't.

Effectiveness of Quantitative Easing Questioned

QE I failed. Will QE II do better? Many economists think not, including Bernanke, having argued (with former Fed vice chairman Alan Blinder) against it in 1988. Minneapolis Fed president Narayana Kocherlakota agrees. Speaking in London in early October 2010, he explained several reasons why, a key one being that banks, flush with reserves, aren't lending.

Pimco's co-CEO Mohamed El-Erian also thinks QE II will fail, headlining on November 4, 2010 in the *Financial Times*, "QE2 blunderbuss likely to backfire," saying:

> ...liquidity injections and financial engineering are insufficient to deal with the challenges that the US faces. Without meaningful structural reforms, part of the Fed's liquidity injection will [cause] another surge of capital flows to other countries...

Precisely what they don't need or want.

Fed policy will force other countries to protect their currencies, perhaps by capital controls, protectionism and other measures. As a result, the dollar's reserve currency status will erode, which is now happening incrementally.

> The unfortunate conclusion is that QE II will be of limited success in sustaining high growth and job creation in the US, and will complicate life for many other countries.

That seems to be what Fed policy intends, wrecking world economies for greater FIRE sector profits and empowerment. Will it work, or will reckless Fed meddling destroy predators with their prey...

Economics Nobel laureate Christopher Pissarides believes QE II won't produce jobs. In a brief comment, economics Nobel laureate Paul Krugman also expressed doubt whether it can work. Former Fed vice chairman Donald Kohn said it won't turn around the US economy. At best, it might help marginally. Economics Nobel laureate Joseph Stiglitz in the *Financial Times* said it's "folly to place all our trust in the Fed," adding:

> It should be obvious that monetary policy has not worked to get the economy out of its current doldrums. [Having failed so far] monetary authorities have turned

to quantitative easing. Even most advocates of monetary policy agree the impact of this is uncertain. What they seldom note, though, are the potential long-term costs.[8]

Stiglitz prefers fiscal over monetary policy, targeting education, technology and infrastructure. Even though government debt will be increased, "the assets on the other side of the balance sheet are increased commensurately," and over time, their return on investment far exceeds the cost. On the other hand, planned austerity, hoping monetary policy can work is "sheer folly." Machiavellian destructiveness better describes it.

Economist David Rosenberg was also skeptical, saying in a November 4, 2010 commentary that he sees QE II having "no visible impact on the willingness to borrow, the money multiplier or velocity, which is what we would need to see to declare this radical policy experiment a success." QE I, in fact, provided none. It was a total flop, suggesting QE II won't fare better. Worse still, Rosenberg saw destructive currency wars intensifying, leading to trade wars that don't "tend to end very well."[9]

Market analyst Bob Chapman calls QE II a futile way to keep the economy and financial system afloat. For one thing, it drives out real investment, "the kind that creates jobs and profits." Fed policies are the opposite, producing debt and speculative excess. In the process, "they also crowd out other borrowers, which ultimately leads to higher interest rates and offsets banks' ability to lend." Moreover, consumers are gravely harmed. Their purchasing power declines, with the economy, as a result, pushed "deeper into depression."[10]

Deflation now besets America, but reckless money creation eventually causes inflation, "to be followed by hyperinflation and ultimately deflationary depression."

George Bernard Shaw observed that "If governments devalue the[ir] currenc[ies] in order to betray all creditors, you politely call this procedure 'inflation.' " It doesn't just happen. It results from reckless monetary and/or fiscal policies.

Moreover, the combination of government-created debt for wars and corporate handouts as well as QE II will "bury the economy." It will do nothing to increase demand, reverse the housing crisis, create jobs, or stimulate growth—which is what sick economies need to get well.

Financial expert and investor safety advocate Martin Weiss worries that the Fed is "unleash(ing) a whole new round of monetary stimulus," potentially driving more liquidity into gold, commodities, foreign currencies, and emerging markets, noting also

one of the greatest disconnects of all time between ...

a sinking economy on the one side, and...the real possibility of roaring bull markets in certain asset classes on the other side.[11]

In his March 21, 2011 commentary, he deplored the exploding federal deficit ($1.7 trillion for FY 2011, underestimated by $2.3 trillion or more over the next decade, according to the Congressional Budget Office) which has the possibility of literally "blowing up like Fukushima, and virtually no one in power has the guts to touch it, let alone expose themselves to the political fallout of actually fixing it."[12] This will result in

- a debased dollar;

- surging food, energy and other commodity prices, much by speculative manipulation;

- steady gold and silver valuation increases;

- eventual "dramatic" interest rate rises, long-term first, then shorter also;

- the destruction of America's middle class;

- an even greater wealth disparity and explosion of poverty;

- disappearance of moderate voices, "accompanied by extreme political polarization between the left and the right;" and

- eventual "fundamental deterioration, even disintegration, in our cultural, social, and political system."

America's leaders, in fact, let conditions spiral out of control. As a result, a grim future awaits.

On November 3, 2010, Bloomberg's Joshua Zumbrun suggested that Republican electoral strength may restrain Fed policy. Don't bet on it. The die is cast. QE II will be unchecked, the announced $600 billion is an amount to be raised freely. Liquidity will flood markets, QEs ad infinitum as long as Fed policy makers dictate it, stopping perhaps only after their house of cards collapses.

At the same time, bipartisan support for austerity portends grave harm to millions of Americans. They're on their own with no help from Washington, with the newly elected bums even worse than the repudiated ones. To their chagrin, voters should now understand how destructive policy harms them, which they already should know with regard to a president and the Democrats who betrayed them.

A Final Comment

QE can work if used constructively, not destructively as planned. Colonial America proved it, Massachusetts first in 1691 with its own paper money, backed by the full faith and credit of the government. Other colonies followed using scrip. It freed them from British banks, and let them grow their economies prosperously, inflation-free, with no taxation for 25 years. The secret lay in not issuing too much, and recycling created money back into local economies for productive growth.

In other words, everything was kept proportionally in balance. Moreover, local governments paid no interest on their own money, which was created for growth, rather than for banker enrichment at the expense of commerce, industry, and the public.

Lincoln did the same thing, again with government created money. His accomplishments and what followed turned America into the world's greatest industrial giant, launching the steel industry, a continental railroad system, a new era of farm machinery and cheap tools.

Free education was also established. The Homestead Act gave settlers ownership rights and encouraged land development. Government supported all branches of science. Mass production methods were standardized. Labor productivity rose up to 75%, and still more was achieved during the post-war years, America's greatest period of growth before the Fed's creation in 1913.

By abolishing or nationalizing it, America could again be sustainably prosperous under a publicly-run banking system, with everyone benefitting from inflation-free growth. Predatory lenders would be eliminated. Too-big-to-fail banks wouldn't exist. Wall Street power would wane or disintegrate because government would control its own money, creating it by making productive investments in the economy, interest-free.

As a result, federal taxes could be reduced or eliminated. Moreover, if states and local communities had their own banks, like North Dakota, it would work as well for them, a topic Chapter 17 addresses.

Under today's privately-run Fed-controlled predatory banking system, Wall Street runs America, wrecking it for its own profit, with QE only its latest scheme. Money creating power could be used productively, but in the hands of the Fed it's a financial WMD, as Warren Buffet himself pointed out. As a result, harder than ever hard times are coming. Only civil action can prevent it, including demanding that government regain control of its own money, as the Constitution's Article 1, Section 8 mandates.

Endnotes

1   Karl Denninger, "America's Alarm Clock Has Rung: Time's Up," *Market Ticker*, available at <http://market-ticker.org/akcs-www?post=171263>

2   James Grant, "Why No Outrage?", *Naked Capitalism*, July 18, 2008, available at <http://www.nakedcapitalism.com/2008/07/jim-grant-why-no-outrage.html>

3   See endnote 1, supra.

4   The Bloomberg interview is available at <http://www.youtube.com/watch?v=26bZVRm4gxM>

5   Michael Hudson, "Bailing Out the Bubble's Enablers," available at <http://www.co-operativeindividualism.org/hudson-michael_housing-crisis-of-2008.html>

6   Available at <http://www.levyinstitute.org/pubs/wp_639.pdf>

7   Id.

8   Joseph Stiglitz, "It is folly to place all our trust in the Fed", *Financial Times*, October 18, 2010.

9   David Rosenberg, "On QEII, The Long-Bond Collapse, and the Next Leg of the Dollar Breakdown", *Business Insider*, Nov. 4, 2010. Available at <http://www.businessinsider.com/david-rosenberg-on-qe2-2010-11>

10   Bob Chapman, "Quantitative Easing (QE2). Debt Created Out of Thin Air: The Crisis in Banking Has Worsened," *GlobalResearch.ca*, September 4, 2010, available at <http://globalresearch.ca/index.php?context=va&aid=20893>

11   Martin Weiss, "Two Game-Changing Decisions," *Money and Markets*, October 18, 2010, at <http://www.moneyandmarkets.com/two-game-changing-decisions-2-40433>

12   Martin Weiss, "Mind-blowing Political Cowardice," *Money and Markets*, March 21, 2011, at <http://www.moneyandmarkets.com/mind-boggling-political-cowardice-43496>

6

FRAUD
IN AMERICA

It's the American way: more for the rich, crumbs for the masses, and fraud as a way of life since the Republic's inception, though hardly on today's scale. Perhaps the first prominent example was in 1792, involving former Assistant Treasury Secretary William Duer. Appointed by Alexander Hamilton in 1789, he left a year later to profit from insider trading, or so he hoped.

At the time, US bonds were junk paper. The market for them was volatile, so profiting meant being savvy enough or tipped off in advance to buy or sell ahead of the news. As a former Treasury official, Duer had insider information. Using leverage, he made it pay handsomely for a while until too much money caused a speculative glut, an earlier type of bubble that took down much of the New York Stock Exchange when it burst, Duer with it.

Way over his head in debt, he nonetheless hung on, expecting to beat the market. But he failed. Instead of getting richer, he went bankrupt, ended up in debtors prison, and Alexander Hamilton had to buy the worthless bonds as the lender of last resort. Sound familiar?

In 1795, Georgia sold 35 million acres of western land to four companies for half a million dollars—less than two cents an acre—in one of America's most corrupt deals ever. By taking bribes for their votes, every member of the legislature, except one, profited, but not for long. Voters caught on, tossing them out at the next election. The fraudulent contract was annulled. In 1802, the federal government bought the land for $1,250,000, but it didn't end there. The Supreme Court got involved, ruling the original deal, though flawed, was legal, forcing Congress to award the claimants over $4 million.

It's a systemic problem, and it's everywhere, especially in savage capitalism's greed-driven system, enriching a global royalty at the expense of most others. In his book, On *Fact and Fraud: Cautionary Tales from the*

Front Lines of Science,[1] David Goodstein examined examples from centuries back to more recent times, including some accusations turning out to be false.

Trinity University's Bob Jensen maintains fraud updates on his website, accessed through the following link:

http://www.trinity.edu/rjensen/FraudUpdates.htm

He also reviewed a "History of Fraud in America," starting in colonial (and pre-colonial) times, saying the earliest kinds involved phony health cures, including snake oil ploys, medical frauds, and other deceptions, transitioning to today's "miracle cures and Internet charlatanism."

Largely agricultural early America was inflicted with land schemes as well as "deceptive rural living and farming products." Con men bought and sold land. Victims were often immigrants and Indians. The one best remembered was the 1626 Manhattan Island purchase "for trinkets valued at 60 guilders," about $24. Ironically in a sense, the Carnarsie Indians were the culprits as their land wasn't part of Manhattan. Usually, however, indigenous people were victimized, with land scams expanding throughout the country west and south, accompanied by other fraud at the expense of the unwary.

Frontier history led to crooked politicians and bureaucrats getting involved, accepting bribes and collaborating with land swindlers. It got worse during corporate America's early days. In 1787, fewer than 40 corporations existed, mostly to build roads, bridges, canals, and other public projects. Many involved "bribes, kickbacks, and inflated prices"—just like today but for smaller stakes.

Corruption and fraud flourished during the Civil War in the form of tainted beef and pork, shoddy blankets and uniforms, knapsacks coming unglued in the rain, guns that blew off soldiers' fingers when firing them, and much more, with war profiteers benefitting handsomely.

During the Gilded Age, a post-Civil War boom, men like Rockefeller in oil, Carnegie in steel, Gould and Vanderbilt in railroads, Morgan in banking, and others profited in the way Vanderbilt explained, saying "What do I care about the law? Hain't I got the power?" Indeed he and others did, through unscrupulous deal-making, buying off politicians, and gaining monopoly power. As Matthew Josephson said in *The Robber Barons*,[2] they were "the ancient barons-of-the-crags—who, by force of arms, instead of corporate combinations, monopolized strategic valley roads or mountain passes through which commerce flowed." They, in fact, controlled commerce and they bought and sold corrupt politicians like commodities.

In *The History of the Standard Oil Company*, Ida Tarbell chronicled one of many, John D. Rockefeller and the colossus he built by circumventing laws and crushing competition ruthlessly.

Mark Twain and Charles Dudley Warner coined the term "gilded age," reflecting the rampant greed, pervasive fraud, corruption, and speculative frenzy during America's greatest ever growth period, creating enormous wealth and corporate power through politically-aided deal-making.

For example, Ulysses S. Grant's administration reeked of graft, mismanagement, and corruption, he and his son going bankrupt from fraudulent investments gone sour. Succeeding administrations were also tainted by letting business entrepreneurs operate freely with little government interference.

They took full advantage, including through insider trading, stock manipulation, and other forms of fraud. In the late 1800s, it enriched men like Jay Gould, James Fisk, Russell Sage, Edward Henry Harriman, JP Morgan, and Daniel Drew. They amassed fortunes from swindling, double-dealing, and other forms of financial chicanery. In Drew's case, however, he died broke in 1879, ruined by fellow manipulators.

Perhaps America's Robber Barons, among others, inspired Honoré de Balzac's maxim that "Behind every great fortune lies a great crime," or words to that effect.

The landmark 1886 case, *Santa Clara County v. Southern Pacific Railroad,* gave corporations personhood under the 14th Amendment. It also helped further proliferate fraud, including stock scams, land grabs, labor exploitation, various types of product and price swindling, and much more.

Now recognized as legal persons with full rights without obligations, corporations were on a roll, heading towards oligopoly or monopoly power— today more than ever, as they operate globally with interlocking directorates, market dominance, and complicit governments arranging things for them.

Years back, General Motors negotiated a major heist with bribes and other means to get cities to abandon street cars for buses. It worked brilliantly, but was disastrous for large communities and the public, forcing them to become more dependent on autos. A sprawling suburbia arose. Urban decay followed, so now ghettos proliferate nationally, with their needs largely ignored.

Prior to the Great Depression, corporations operated virtually regulation free. That changed, but over time consumer protections were eroded. Thereafter, global cartels arranged business-friendly environments, manipulated them for profit, and committed greater than ever fraud. It's worst of all on Wall Street, especially after the 1913 Federal Reserve Act gave big banks money creation power, letting them game the system more than ever, including giving them a free hand to commit fraud.

The 1920s stock selling scandals culminated in the 1929 crash, the Great Depression, New Deal reforms, WW II, post-war prosperity, leading to the late 1960s-1970s excesses, turbulence and inflation, proving what goes around comes around.

Reaganomics and 1980s deregulation then facilitated the savings and loan fraud, junk bonds, leveraged buyouts, greenmailing, Boesky, Milken, Dennis Levine, then crime on the order of Enron, Worldcom, Madoff, other Ponzi schemes, neoliberalism, globalization, market manipulation, bubbles, derivatives flimflam, embezzling, insider trading, false accounting, phony financial products, misrepresentation, other scams, conspiracies, and "foreclosuregate."

Fraudulent Forceclosures

Massive fraud is involved—forged documents, fabricated and backdated ones, perjury, lost paperwork, and false affidavits, causing millions of mortgage defaults, with owners evicted after their properties have been seized illegally.

William K. Black is a lawyer, academic, former S & L regulator, and author of *The Best Way to Rob a Bank Is to Own One: How Corporate Executives and Politicians Looted the S & L Industry*. He and Economics Professor L. Randall Wray also co-wrote an article titled, "Foreclose on the Foreclosure Fraudsters, Part I: Put Bank of America in Receivership,"[3] saying that overwhelming evidence shows "the entire foreclosure process is riddled with fraud, [yet] President Obama refuses to support a national moratorium," making him conspiratorially complicit in a huge scandal, ravaging millions of homeowners lawlessly. Protecting bankers, not victims, is policy, so coverup and denial of systemic fraud persists.

Moreover, "despite our pleas, the FBI has continued its 'partnership' with the Mortgage Bankers Association (MBA)...the trade association of the 'perps.' It created a ridiculous...definition of 'mortgage fraud,' [saying] lenders—who [created them]—are the victims. The FBI" plays ball. That's why no one's been prosecuted nor likely will be, except perhaps some lower level officials taking a fall for their bosses, with the top executives continuing to profit hugely by scamming innocent victims who are hung out to dry.

In fact, criminal CEOs "looted with impunity, were left in power, and were granted their fondest wish when Congress...extorted the professional Financial Accounting Standards Board (FASB) to turn the accounting rules into a farce." It let banks "refuse to recognize hundreds of billions of losses, [produce fake] 'income' and 'capital,' " so the fraudsters got richer than ever.

Black and Wray want it stopped by "prompt corrective action," halting foreclosures until corrective steps are taken and "financial institutions that committed widespread fraud [are put] in receivership," replacing their bosses with honest, competent officials, if any can be found at a time of unbridled, anything-goes greed.

Along with Goldman Sachs, JPMorgan Chase, Citigroup, and Wells Fargo, Bank of America tops the list; all are criminal enterprises, operating with government complicity. Besides B of A's other chicanery, its books reek with "many billions of dollars of fraudulent loans originated by Countrywide," its 2009 acquisition.

Countrywide is symbolic of banking industry racketeering, selling "hundreds of thousands of fraudulent loans through false reps and warranties," most then illegally foreclosed. Like other mortgage scammers, it victimized hundreds of thousands of people and hundreds of counterparties, causing massive losses, with homeowners, of course, hit hardest. In fact, Countrywide "defrauded more people, at a greater cost, than any entity in history."

But other mortgage lenders contributed their share as part of a giant con game against the public from which they keep profiting, scooping up foreclosed properties on the cheap, then defrauding new unwary buyers when they resold properties they don't own because the entire scheme is fraudulent. It means evicted owners deserve their homes back, but try winning their case in court when right-wing judges back business, not justice.

Analyst Bob Chapman explained:

> The fraud committed by the foreclosure mills, at the behest of the banks, puts all foreclosures into question and even the status of those homeowners who are currently paying their mortgages. That means if homeowners all stop paying their mortgages, they could end up owning their homes. This is a mega crisis far bigger that Bear Stearns and Lehman...[4]

But even bigger ones are coming after years of systemic fraud, the extent of which is staggering.

As for housing, Chapman said:

> Foreclosures are now one in 12. Four years ago it was 1 in 100. For sure home prices have not bottomed. It could be the mortgage market is dead and all the bondholders are sunk. [If true, the nation's] financial structure is close to collapse.

Countrywide did much to cause it. According to Black and Wray, its top executives were "infamous," yet B of A made them senior leaders, and administration officials "trivialize (their) criminality," refusing to hold them and others accountable for obvious reasons: because they, and earlier administrations, helped engineer the housing bubble since the mid-1990s. Though now the housing market is deflating, victims continue being scammed.

So instead of fixing the problem and aiding homeowners, the situation festers, grows, and lets "too-big-to-fail" systemically dangerous institutions (SDIs) get bigger, creating greater than ever risks. As a result, we're literally "rolling the dice with disaster every day," with world economies held hostage by powerful banks.

The obvious solution is avoided—placing B of A and other insolvent banks in receivership, breaking them up, replacing and prosecuting their culpable officials, and restructuring a dysfunctional system into a workable one, excluding predatory banks.

Ellen Brown does some of the best financial writing around. In 2010, she covered foreclosure swindling involving fabricated documents, forgery, and perjury, proliferating massive fraud, including lost paperwork that "would have revealed to investors that they had been sold a bill of goods—a package of toxic subprime loans very prone to default."[5] Yet they were cleverly dressed up in legal mumbo jumbo to resemble AAA quality until post-bubble foreclosures exposed the scam, too late to save most victims.

On October 7, 2010, *Washington Post* writers Brady Dennis and Ariana Eunjung headlined, "In foreclosure controversy, problems run deeper than flawed paperwork," saying: "Millions of US mortgages have been shuttled around the global financial system—sold and resold by firms—without the documents that traditionally prove who legally owns the loans." With millions now in default and homes seized, "judges around the country have increasingly ruled that lenders had no right to foreclose, because they lacked clear title."[6]

In fact, major US banks faked documents to speed up foreclosures illegally—a criminal industry with Washington partnership dispossessing defrauded homeowners from their properties. In other words, when pols conspire with Wall Street racketeers, the public gets scammed, in this case, millions of victimized homeowners.

In September 2010, "foreclosuregate" emerged after evidence forced Ally Financial (formerly GMAC Mortgage) to stop dispossessions in 23 states where court orders are needed.

At issue are backdated documents, false affidavits, and so-called court-ordered "rocket docket" speed-throughs to evict homeowners, with proceedings lasting around 20 seconds per case. Judges are so swamped, they pay no attention," said Margery Golant, a veteran Florida foreclosure defense lawyer. As a result, "They just rubber-stamp them,"[7] case closed.

On October 8, 2010, Bank of America announced it would halt foreclosure sales in all 50 states. Earlier, Ally Financial and JPMorgan Chase said they were doing so in 23 states. PNC Financial Services Group also did so for 30 days. Other banks followed, only, however, for the short-term before resuming government-sanctioned racketeering, and again throwing people into the street for profit. When green-lighted by Washington, anything goes.

On October 8, 2010, Obama pocket-vetoed a rushed-through Senate bill to facilitate foreclosure fraud. It would have mandated that mortgage and other financial document notarizations done in one state (including those done electronically) be recognized in all others. Consumer groups and other critics complained, saying the measure would have facilitated dispossessions faster, and in many cases improperly.

Attorney General Eric Holder at the time said the Financial Fraud Enforcement Task Force is investigating reports of greater numbers. Seven or more state attorneys general began their own investigations, which if not stopping, at least may slow down dispossessions. More on that below.

In May 2010, Herman John Kennerty, a Wells Fargo default document group administration manager testified that he typically signed 50 to 150 evictions daily. He also said he didn't independently verify information to which he was attesting, just rubber-stamped it along.

In Florida, problems have been especially acute. In fact, the 12th Judicial Circuit state findings showed 20% of foreclosures set for summary judgment involved deficient documents, according to Chief Judge Lee E. Haworth. In an interview, he said:

> We have sent repeated notices to law firms saying, 'You are not following the rules, and if you don't clean up your act, we are going to impose sanctions on you.' They say, 'We'll fix it, we'll fix it, we'll fix it.' But they don't.

As a result, on September 17, 2010, Judge Harry Rapkin, overseeing district foreclosures, dismissed 61 cases. Plaintiffs may refile, however, by repeating the procedure, including paying fees involved.

Overall, the process is riddled with fraud. Mortgage lenders used boiler room tactics, conning borrowers with no knowledge of what they were doing, including the risks. To close deals, some forged their signatures on key documents, pressured real estate appraisers to inflate home values, and created fake W-2 forms to exaggerate applicant incomes.

Workable Alternatives

In her extraordinary book, *Web of Debt*, Brown explained how private bankers usurped money creation power, and how we can get it back. Providing more information, her October 21, 2010 article titled, "Repairing a Dysfunctional Banking System," said that stopping financial predators depends on "turning banking into a public utility, one that advances the credit of the community," and not third party criminal enterprises pretending to be legitimate. Today, it's worse than ever. Brown quotes Ann Pettifor, a fellow of the London-based New Economics Foundation, saying:

> [T]he banking system is now fully dysfunctional. It has failed in its primary purpose: to act as a machine for lending into the real economy. Instead [it's] become a borrowing machine...from the real economy, and then refusing to lend, except at high rates of interest, [effectively] lobotom[izing] the real economy.

Unemployment and poverty keep rising, and millions of homeowners are losing their most precious asset, mostly by criminal fraud. "Our homes," said Brown, "have become pawns in a great pawn shop run for the benefit of large institutional investors and the banks that profit from them. Our [securitized] sliced and diced houses are the chips moved around in a global casino," the model having "crashed against the hard rock of hundreds of years of state real estate law [with] requirements" banks haven't met, and can't meet "if they are to comply with the tax laws for mortgage-backed securities."

The name of the game is fraud, outright categorical massive theft because that's how the system is structured. Banks aren't creating credit responsibly. They are, in fact, "vacuuming up our own money and lending it back to us at higher rates," including usurious ones on credit cards.

They're "sucking up our real estate and lending it back to our pension (and) mutual funds at compound interest. The result is a mathematically impossible pyramid scheme," inherently prone to fail.

It's flawed, fraudulent, and essential to replace. Brown proposes a "public credit solution" through publicly-owned banks—"a public utility operated for the benefit of" communities nationwide, returning profits to the locales where they were generated, not to a Wall Street crime syndicate.

Since 1919, North Dakota has been the precedent-setting model as the nation's only state-owned bank, the BND. Sustained by its distinctiveness and strength, it's been a credit machine, delivering productive financial services for agriculture, commerce and industry that no other state can match because they don't have state-owned banks—but easily could.

Chapter 17 explains the BND model more fully, its success, and why all states could prosper like North Dakota with their own state-owned banks.

North Dakota offers a workable alternative, a public ownership way for everyone, lifting all boats fairly and equitably, instead of bilking the many for the few, and wrecking America in the process.

It's also a way to stop future bipartisan-facilitated grandest of grand theft bailouts, letting America's Treasury be looted of trillions of dollars, as government partners with bankers for plunder, sucking up public wealth for Wall Street crooks.

Underlying Causes of Fraud in America

Bob Jensen listed eight on his website mentioned above, including:

- an obsession with privacy, freedom being "prized over the risk of being ripped off;"

- laws and courts go easy on white collar criminals, the worst of them rich/well-connected crooks escaping punishment unlike what blue collar or violent crime perpetrators face;

- whistleblowing is discouraged, and doing it is a high-risk undertaking because lawsuits and other types of retaliation may follow, including ostracism by fellow employees;

- declining morality and ethics at a time of extreme unregulated greed;

- unaccountable contracting, auditors dealing with complex financial deals "so complicated that they virtually cannot be (properly) audited or explained;"

- as a result, "incompetent and corrupt audits are routine...the audit trail end[ing] in front of a maze of networked computers or some giant black box that cannot be fathomed;"

- CPA audits have flawed designs, with firms doing them in jeopardy of losing clients unless they issue "clean" reports, and rating agencies facing the same challenge, play ball or else; and

- money corrupting politics, forcing candidates to seek out large donors for campaigns in return for which friendly legislation and deregulation follow.

As a result, ever larger, more sophisticated fraud schemes proliferate. They "roll across America like waves move onto a beach. [They] rise and fall with new innovations and ultimate corrections." Creative corporate ploys follow new accounting and auditing rules, exponentially growing to become nearly incomprehensible.

So far, corporate bad guys are winning, their excesses continuing unrestrained. Neither legislation, potential lawsuits, nor criminal prosecutions deter them. The "weakest front" is the political one because office holders need cash, and powerful lobbyists game the system for them. So one scandal begets another, with the new ones increasingly greater for larger stakes. Big money always prevails while consumer households lose out.

The Housing Bubble

The housing bubble was no accident. It was built on an edifice of fraud, according to Catherine Austin Fitts, a former Assistant Housing Secretary. From 1994-1997, her company, Hamilton Securities, was the lead Federal Housing Administration (FHA) advisor. An expert, she "watched both the Administration and the Federal Reserve [game the system by] aggressively implement[ing] the policies that engineered the housing bubble."

In her March 15, 2009 *Solari.com* article headlined, "The Fed Did Indeed Cause the Housing Bubble," she explained:

> In 1995, a senior Clinton Administration official shared with me the Administration's targets for Fannie Mae and Freddie Mac mortgage volumes in low and moderate-income communities. We had recently reviewed the Administration's plans to increase government mortgage guarantees—and most of these mortgages would also be pooled and sold as securities to investors.
> Even in 1995, I could see that these plans would create unserviceable debt loads in communities struggling with the falling incomes expected from globalization. Homeowners would default on mortgages while losses on mortgage-backed securities would drain retirement savings from 401(k)s and pension plans. Taxpayers would ultimately be hit with a large bill... but insiders would make a bundle. I looked at the official and said that the Administration was planning on issuing more mortgages than there were houses or residents.[8]

The response she got was, "Shut up, this is none of your business."

In her August 7, 2007 article titled, "Sub-Prime Mortgage Woes Are No Accident," Fitts wrote:

> One of the dirty little secrets behind the housing bubble is the longstanding partnership [between] narcotics trafficking and mortgage fraud, [both used] to target and destroy minority and poor communities with highly profitable economic warfare.[9]

More on the Financial Meltdown

On May 6, 2009, the Center for Public Integrity headlined, "Who's Behind the Financial Meltdown: The Top 25 Subprime Lenders and Their Wall Street Backers,"[10] saying the companies most responsible "for triggering the global economic meltdown were owned or backed by giant banks now collecting billions of dollars in bailout money." Trillions actually, the precise number not known because Washington won't reveal it.

Profiteering banks include Goldman Sachs, JPMorgan Chase, Bank of America, Citigroup, Wells Fargo, and other familiar names, which were benefitting hugely through criminally engineered fraud, facilitated by government—initially during the Clinton administration, or perhaps earlier. For sure, the Reagan and Bush I administrations also reeked of corruption and scandals.

Banks getting bailout money, in fact, own, financed, or were financially connected to at least 21 of the top subprime lenders. Twenty have now closed, stopped lending, or were sold to avoid bankruptcy. Nine were California based, including: Countrywide Financial, Ameriquest Mortgage, New Century Financial, First Franklin, and Long Beach Mortgage, scamming homebuyers through criminal fraud.

State Foreclosure Fraud Investigations

As explained above, seven or more state attorneys general began investigations, and reports suggest up to 40 or more may work cooperatively on it. According to *Bloomberg.com* on October 8, 2010:

> State attorneys general led by Iowa's Tom Miller are in talks that may lead to the announcement of a coordinated probe as soon as October 12... Lawyers representing the banks are expecting a more widespread investigation, according to Patrick McManemin, a partner at Patton Boggs, a Washington-based law firm that represents banks, loan servicers and financial institutions.[11]

Lawsuits may follow. At least one has been initiated by Ohio Attorney General Richard Cordray against Ally Financial, formerly GMAC Mortgage.

Whether Attorney General Holder and top congressional officials will get on this forcefully remains to be seen. So far, there's more furor than action or tough measures. It had already subsided post-election, given other lame duck session priorities, then a new Congress in January focused on austerity for working households to fund corporate favorites and imperial wars, the way the system always works. However, the housing scandal is so huge ("foreclosuregate" is just one part alone) that momentum may give it legs for many months, if only because millions of homeowners are affected.

The situation bears watching. Financial institutions may be penalized, but expect no top heads to roll, perhaps only some lower-level sacrificial lambs. It's how Washington officials always handle scandals, because they, too, are complicit and would face consequences.

Global Drugs Trafficking: Profiteering from Destroying Poor Communities

The model is global, profiting hugely from illicit drugs, money laundering, and economic destruction of poor communities. Business, government, and CIA officials at the highest levels are involved because of the enormous stakes.

In 2003, the IMF estimated global money laundering at between $590 billion--$1.5 trillion annually through major financial firms, mostly in America. In fact, $500 billion alone comes from the illicit (US-controlled) Afghanistan opium trade (plus tens of millions more from hashish), most of it laundered through US and European banks, mainly the largest, but others as well, worldwide.

In his books, *Cocaine Politics and Drugs, Oil and War* and *American War Machine: Deep Politics, the CIA Global Drug Connection, and the Road to Afghanistan*, as well as other writings, Peter Dale Scott provided detailed information on the CIA-drugs connection. In one article, he states: "Since at least 1950 there has been a global CIA-drug connection operating more or less continuously," relating to numerous "deep events" like JFK's assassination, the 1964 Gulf of Tonkin incident, Iran-Contra, and the CIA's involvement with the mob, and used for "supportive counterviolence... where Communist forces have appeared strong."[12]

> The global drug connection is not just a lateral connection between CIA field operatives and their drug-trafficking contacts. It is more significantly a global financial complex of hot money uniting prominent business, financial and government as well as underworld figures, [a sort of] indirect empire [subverting] existing government...[13]

Iran-Contra is just one of many examples.

Today, it's likely more virulent than ever, perhaps topping $2 trillion annually. Like the housing bubble, foreclosuregate, and numerous other scams, innocent millions are ripped off for profit, aided and abetted by government complicity.

Ignoring Bernie Madoff's Scam

Whistleblower Harry Markopolos tried unsuccessfully to expose Madoff. On November 7, 2005, his 21-page document to the SEC explained that "The World's Largest [Madoff-run] Hedge Fund is a Fraud." He collected "first-hand observations" from fund-of-fund Madoff investors and heads of Wall Street equity derivative trading desks. Every senior manager called Madoff a fraud.

Markopolos, in fact, is a "derivatives expert" with experience in the strategy he used. He said "[v]ery few people [anywhere] have the mathematical background needed to manage these types of products," but he's one of them.

He listed "Red Flags" that were making him suspicious that "Madoff's returns [weren't] real." Because careers and his own safety were at risk, his report was unsigned, written solely for internal SEC use. He suggested the "highly likely" possibility that "Madoff Securities is the world's largest Ponzi Scheme," but he worried about his powerful political connections.

Markopolos' 29 Red Flags included the following:

- why did Madoff Securities (BM) charge only undisclosed commissions on trades and not operate like other hedge funds—taking a 1% management fee + 20% of the profits;

- why did Madoff not let hedge and fund-of-fund investors mention his firm's name in their performance summaries or marketing literature; why the secrecy—any money manager with great returns would want all the publicity he or she could get;

- Madoff's split-strike strategy was inferior to an "all index approach," thus "incapable" of consistently high returns; in fact, he shouldn't have been able to beat safe Treasury yields;

- BM's protection "put" option buying strategy hurts returns; it should have challenged him to earn average 0% ones, not the spectacular performance he achieved;

- given the estimated size of his assets, "there [weren't] enough index option put contracts in existence to hedge the way BM" claimed; his strategy was mathematically impossible;

- counterparty credit exposure for firms like UBS and Merrill Lynch were too large for these companies to approve;

- his high returns could only be generated by so-called "front-running" his customers' order flows, using advance information unavailable to others; the practice is illegal and those using it are guilty of securities fraud.

Markopolos concluded, saying:

> I am pretty confident that BM is a Ponzi Scheme, but in the off chance he is front-running orders and his returns are real, then this case qualifies as insider trading under the SEC's bounty program as outlined in Section 21A(e) of [The Securities Exchange Act of 1934]... However, if BM was front-running, a highly profitable activity, then he wouldn't need to borrow funds from investors at 16% implied interest. Therefore it is far more likely that [this was] a Ponzi Scheme...The elaborateness of [his] secrecy, his high 16% average cost of funds, and reliance on a derivatives investment scheme that few investors (or regulators) could be capable of comprehending [provide strong evidence] that this [was] a Ponzi Scheme [and Madoff was a swindler]. [14]

In May 1999, Markopolos alerted the SEC's Boston office of his suspicions, urged it investigate, and followed up with repeated futile requests until the New York office (on January 4, 2006) got involved, based on his allegations.

As a result, the SEC learned plenty but didn't act, even though it discovered that Madoff:

- personally "misled the examination staff about the nature of his" Fairfield and other hedge fund accounts strategy;

- failed to inform his Fairfield funds investors that he was the investment advisor; and

- violated rules requiring that investment advisors register with the SEC; they must do so if they have more than 15 clients.

Using Markopolos' documents, the SEC also investigated his allegations of front-running and Ponzi scheme practices, concluded they weren't substantiated, and recommended closing the case because Madoff "agreed to register his investment advisory business and Fairfield agreed to disclose information about Mr. Madoff to investors."

It justified its action, saying that the "violations [it uncovered] were not so serious as to warrant an enforcement action." In fact, it was clear due diligence negligence, giving a Wall Street insider a free pass. It's very typical of how the SEC operates.

In early 2008, Markopolos tried again through the SEC's Washington office after getting an email from Jonathan Sokobin, an official charged with searching for big market risks. With low expectations, he responded by emailing a very strong subject line: "$30 billion Equity Derivative Hedge Fund Fraud in New York." He cited an unnamed Wall Street pro who recently redeemed money from Madoff after learning that supposed trades in his account weren't made.

Sokobin never responded. Markopolos heard nothing further for months until a friend said Madoff had been arrested.

He was vindicated. "I kept firing bigger and bigger bullets at Madoff, but couldn't stop him. I finally felt relief"—no thanks to the SEC and Wall Street's culture of fraud, with big fish protecting each other because they all do similar things of one sort or other, while the SEC acts more as facilitator than regulator.

Former SEC examiner of advisors and funds Eric Bright explained:

> It wouldn't be the first time that something [like the Madoff case] fell through the cracks. The revolving [SEC] door is the biggest problem. Many staff regulators who are ambitious and competent quit to pursue jobs in the financial industry that pay multiple times their government salaries.
>
> During my time at the SEC, I heard the excuses about why cases that we, the examination staff, uncovered failed to warrant actions by the enforcement staff. Too small...too complicated...too politically connected, don't rock the boat...It is time to rethink the structure of the regulatory system because what we have isn't working.

SEC Non-Enforcement Under George Bush

During Bush's tenure, federal stock fraud investigations dropped sharply, making the SEC more ineffective than ever.

According to a Syracuse University research group analysis, Department of Justice prosecutions dropped from 437 cases in 2000 to 133 through November 30, 2008. At the SEC, it was worse, investigations dropping from 69 in 2000 to seven in 2007—an 87% due diligence decline.

Jacob Zamansky, a New York lawyer specializing in representing aggrieved investors, said "the SEC completely fell down on the job. They're more interested in protecting Wall Street than individuals." The agency needs a complete overhaul. Chances were slim then and now.

Former New York prosecutor Sean Coffey agreed, calling SEC's enforcement efforts "awful." It "neutered the ability of the enforcement staff to be as proactive as they could be. It's hard to square the motto of investor advocate with the way they've performed the last eight years." It's little different today under Obama despite a proposed FY 2012 budget increase. It may or may not be approved, but will hardly matter either way, given the prevailing culture of impunity.

Since Ronald Reagan, under Democrat and Republican administrations, Wall Street enjoyed a free ride. Foxes guard the hen house. Regulators don't regulate. Investigations aren't conducted. Criminal fraud goes undetected. Little is done to eliminate it, and, except for rare instances like Bernie Madoff, (forced to confess because his house of cards collapsed), only small offenders need worry.

Section 4 of the Securities Exchange Act of 1934 established the SEC. It's mandated to enforce the Securities Act of 1933, the Trust Indenture Act of 1939, the 1940 Investment Company Act and Investment Advisers Act, Sarbanes-Oxley of 2002, and the Credit Rating Agency Reform Act of 2006. Overall, it's responsible for enforcing federal securities laws, the securities industry, the nation's stock and options exchanges, and other electronic securities markets. It's charged with uncovering wrongdoing, assuring investors aren't swindled, and keeping the nation's financial markets free from fraud.

It has five commissioners, a chairman, four main divisions (Corporation Finance, Trading and Markets, Investment Management, and Enforcement), 11 regional offices, a large staff and budget, and increasingly, a culture of non-enforcement.

Madoff is another black eye for SEC lack of due diligence. Many others happened earlier, including a former enforcement chief tipping off a private lawyer about an impending insider trading inquiry.

Another example involved the agency's Miami office where investigators inexplicably dropped an important inquiry involving securities sold by Bear Stearns (BS). A third instance documented the lack of any significant oversight over BS in the months leading to its collapse.

SEC's enforcement division, in fact, was hampered by Bush administration budget cuts and regulatory changes, making it harder to impose penalties, even in cases of egregious wrongdoing. Other problems still remain, including accusations that its employees engage in illegal insider trading and falsify financial disclosure forms. Moreover, officials repeatedly don't investigate, especially against Wall Street giants, which are practically licensed to steal with impunity, with nothing other than occasional minor hand slaps, which are doing nothing to deter them. [15]

Mary Schapiro now heads the SEC for Obama. Chapter 11 discusses her longstanding industry ties, assuring friendly non-enforcement on her watch.

A Notorious Non-Financial Scandal

It involved the Exxon Valdez incident after the March 24, 1989 spill ravaged Alaska's Prince William Sound and Lower Cook Inlet, ruining the livelihoods of area fishermen and residents. Lawsuits followed:

- In September 1994, $287 million in compensatory damages and $5 billion in punitive ones were awarded;

- In December 2002, the Ninth Circuit US Court of Appeals reduced the latter to $4 billion;

- In December 2006, after more appeals, the same court cut another $1.5 billion; and

- In June 2008, the US Supreme Court reduced punitive damages to $500 million—the equivalent of about 1.5 days profit from ExxonMobil's first quarter 2008 operations. No company executive went to jail for what was up to that time the worst environmental crime in history. It was whitewashed for 10 cents on the dollar after nearly 20 years of litigation.

Years from now, expect final resolution of Gulf of Mexico destruction (a far greater crime than Exxon's) to be similar, with oil giant BP at most paying pennies for every dollar's worth of destruction caused by far the greatest ever environmental crime, which is still harming millions who'll never be compensated for their losses, including to their heath and futures.

Endnotes

1   David Goodstein, *On Fact and Fraud: Cautionary Tales from the Front Lines of Science*, Princeton University Press, 2010.
2   Mathew Josephson, *The Robber Barons*, Mariner Books, 1962.
3   Available at <http://www.michaelmoore.com/words/mike-friends-blog/foreclose-foreclosure-fraudsters-part-1-put-bank-america-receivership>
4   Bob Chapman, "The Securitization Scam: Foreclosures and the Mortgage Electronic Registration Systems (MERS)" GlobalResearch.ca, October 23, 2010, available at <http://globalresearch.ca/index.php?context=va&aid=21585>
5   Ellen Brown, "Foreclosuregate", webofdebt.com, October 7, 2010, available at <http://www.webofdebt.com/articles/foreclosuregate.php>
6   Available at <http://www.washingtonpost.com/wp-dyn/content/article/2010/10/06/

AR2010100607227.html>

7   Gretchen Morgenson and Geraldine Fabrikant, "Florida's High-Speed Answer to a Foreclosure Mess", *The New York Times*, September 4, 2010.

8   Available at <http://www.globalresearch.ca/index.php?context=va&aid=12858>

9   Catherine Austin Fitts, "The Fed Did Indeed Cause the Housing Bubble," *The Solari Report Blog*, March 15, 2009, available at < http://solari.com/blog/?p=2293>

10   Available at < http://www.publicintegrity.org/investigations/economic_meltdown/>

11   Dakin Campbell and Prashant Gopal, "Attorneys General in 40 States Said to Join on Foreclosures", *Bloomberg.com,* October 8, 2010. Available at <http://www.bloomberg.com/news/2010-10-08/attorneys-general-in-40-states-said-to-join-on-foreclosures.html>

12   Peter Dale Scott, "Deep Events and the CIA's Global Drug Connection," *GlobalResearch.ca*, August 17, 2008. The full article with endnotes is available at <globalresearch.ca/articles/PeterDaleScott.doc>

13   Id.

14   See "Harry Markopolous / Markopolos Letter to the SEC 2005, against Madoff," available at <http://www.unanimocracy.com/featured/harry-markopolous-markopolos-letter-to-the-sec-2005-against-madoff/>

15   Approximately 45 per cent of institutional investors felt that better oversight by the SEC could have prevented the Madoff fraud." Stated at InvestmentLaw.us, at http://www.investmentlaw.us/United_States_Securities_and_Exchange_Commission/encyclopedia.htm citing "Little faith in regulators and rating agencies, as LP demand for alternatives cools off, finds survey". <http://www.briskfox.com/open/years/2009_q1/do_h_c44818.php.> (No longer available).

OBAMA'S ANTI-POPULIST BUDGET AND DEFICIT FIX

Despite its flaws and failures during America's Great Depression, FDR's New Deal was remarkable for what it accomplished. It helped people, put millions back to work, reinvigorated the national spirit, built or renovated 700,000 miles of roads, 7,800 bridges, 45,000 schools, 2,500 hospitals, 13,000 parks and playgrounds, 1,000 airfields, and various other infrastructure, including much of Chicago's lakefront where this writer lives. It cut unemployment from 25% in May 1933 to 11% in 1937, before declaring victory too early and letting it spike before early war production revived economic growth and headed it lower.

Moreover, key New Deal legislation included:

- the landmark 1935 Social Security Act—to this day, the single most important federal program keeping millions of seniors from poverty or easing it for those already poor;

- unemployment insurance in partnership with states;

- two "Soak the Rich" revenue acts to make high earners pay more, another targeting tax cheats, and one taxing undistributed corporate profits;

- the landmark Wagner Act, letting labor, for the first time, bargain collectively with management;

- Glass-Steagall, separating commercial from investment banks and insurance companies, among other provisions to curb speculation;

- public housing and low financing measures;

- other initiatives to reform and revive the economy.

Had Franklin D. Roosevelt lived in good health, perhaps a second bill of rights would have come into being, an economic one he proposed, but died before being able to fulfill it. Saying the first one fell short, he wanted guarantees for:

- full employment with a living wage;

- freedom from unfair competition and monopolies;

- housing;

- medical care;

- education; and

- greater social security, providing more than his landmark act.

Obama's No FDR

Obama's agenda lets Wall Street loot the treasury, rewards other corporate favorites generously, ignores vital people's needs, does little to create jobs or help homeowners facing foreclosure, and spends up to $1.5 trillion annually on unbridled militarism and imperial wars at a time when America has no enemies.

Now the latest—his proposed anti-populist FY 2012 budget that Republicans and right wing pundits say doesn't go far enough.

On February 14, *New York Times* writer Jackie Calmes headlined, "Obama's Budget Focuses on Path to Rein in Deficit," saying it "address[es] the deficit and the best path to long-term economic success... [H]e laid out a path for bringing down annual deficits to more sustainable levels over the rest of the decade," saying he'll reduce it "over the next decade by $1.1 trillion, or about 10%," and it's only for starters.

Much more is planned, targeting entitlements once thought untouchable, including Social Security, Medicare and Medicaid. They're heading for the chopping block and toward elimination along with public pensions, robbing millions of vital protections and futures to do more for America's super-rich and facilitate imperial global rampaging.

That's Obama's real agenda—soaking working households and the poor, transferring greater wealth to America's super-rich who already have too much, and continuing lawless imperial wars and other interventions for unchallengeable global dominance.

Nonetheless, House Budget Committee chairman Paul Ryan accused Obama of "an abdication of leadership" for not doing more on the backs of working and poor households the way he and other Republicans propose, letting America's aristocracy get richer.

A same day *Times* editorial headlined, "The Obama Budget," saying:

> On paper, President Obama's new $3.7 trillion budget is encouraging. It makes a number of tough choices to cut the deficit...which is enough to prevent an uncontrolled explosion of debt in the next decade and, as a result, reduce the risk of a fiscal crisis. [It's] balanced enough to start the process of deficit reduction, but not so draconian that it would derail the recovery. [It's] a good starting point for discussion...

Wall Street Journal writers want more, as featured in a lead February 15, 2011 editorial headlined, "The Cee Lo Green Budget," calling it "cynical and unrealistic," saying: "...what landed on Congress's doorstep on Monday was a White House budget that increases deficits above the spending baseline for the next two years. Hosni Mubarak was more in touch with reality last Thursday night," mindless, in fact, that Mubarak didn't fall. He was pushed, with Washington and Egypt's military forced into doing the shoving. "How unserious is this budget," asked *Journal* writers?

Targeting most cuts after 2016, Obama proposed "Budget Flimfam 101."

Obama: Corporate/Imperial Tool

Whether now, later or in between, Obama's budget hammers working Americans, especially those poor, forgotten, vulnerable, and ignored since Reagan succeeded Carter. Democrats have been as cruel as Republicans, serving wealth and power interests alone while pretending to care.

Weeks after capitulating to Republicans on tax cuts for America's super-rich and corporations, adding hundreds of billions to the deficit, Obama now wants funding reductions for:

- the Low Income Home Energy Assistance Program (LIHEAP) that provides billions to states to help families heat or cool homes; in FY 2010, 8.3 million households needed it, especially to avoid freezing in winter;

- Pell Grants, providing millions of dollars for higher education, what Kris Wright, University of Minnesota director of student finance, calls the "granddaddy of all [student] financial aid programs," crucial to help low-income students attend school;

- the Children's Health Insurance Program (CHIP);

- community healthcare centers;

- nonprofit health insurance cooperatives;

- HIV/AIDS, tuberculosis, and other disease prevention programs;

- WIC (Women, Infants, and Children) grants to states for supplemental foods, healthcare, and nutrition education for low-income families;

- Head Start, providing comprehensive education, health, nutrition, and parent involvement services to low-income families with children;

- the Supplemental Nutrition Assistance Program (targeted earlier with more coming), providing food stamps for poor households;

- community development block grants for housing, overall reducing HUD's budget by $1.1 billion;

- Federal Emergency Management Agency (FEMA) first-responder funding;

- energy efficiency and renewable energy programs;

- Environmental Protection Agency (EPA) clean/safe water and other projects;

- National Institutes of Health (NIH) medical research;

- the National Park Service;

- vital infrastructure and transportation needs;

- other non-defense discretionary spending.

He's cutting vital programs in order to sustain militarism, favoritism, waste, fraud, and other rewards for Washington's usual special interests, benefitting greatly at the public trough.

Social spending cuts now and ahead will facilitate that. On February 5, 2011, Obama's budget director, Jacob Lew, signaled what's planned in his *New York Times* op-ed headlined, "The Easy Cuts Are Behind Us," saying: "... to make room for the investments we need to foster growth, we have to cut what we cannot afford," meaning longstanding social services millions rely on, need, and will face grave hardships if lost. They're coming to "prepare the United States to win in the world economy" at the expense of most of its citizens, sacrificed for elitist interests, the usual ones lined up for more.

Obama's Draconian Deficit Fix

Besides what's covered above, Obama's 12-year deficit reduction program includes:

- $4 trillion cut overall;

- $770 billion from education, environmental, transportation, and other infrastructure cuts, as well as lower wages and benefits for federal workers when they need more, not less;

- $480 billion from Medicare and Medicaid, besides another $1 trillion from Obamacare;

- $360 billion from mandated domestic programs, including food stamps, home heating assistance, income for the poor and disabled, federal pension insurance, and farm subsidies;

- $400 billion from military-related spending from unneeded weapons, as well as healthcare and other benefits for active service members and veterans—not priority items the Pentagon and war profiteers want to protect like generous annual defense spending increases and supplemental add-ons, plus black-hole black budgets for intelligence and other nefarious purposes.

Like all his demagoguery since taking office, Obama hypocrically says we're broke and must make "shared sacrifices." In fact, he suppresses how he's served wealth and power interests at the expense of working Americans during the greatest economic crisis since the Great Depression, making workers sacrifice so elitists get more to share.

A Final Comment

Chapter 12 discusses equitable alternatives far different than Obama proposed. The alternative includes imperial lawlessness, endemic corruption, high unemployment, growing impoverishment, social inequality and decay, unmet human needs, and eroding freedoms, heading America toward tyranny and ruin the way all past empires declined and fell. Republican or Democrat proposals will hasten it, unless challenged and stopped.

8

THE RECESSION
IS OVER
THE DEPRESSION
IS JUST BEGINNING

In late 2009, economist David Rosenberg said the following:

The credit collapse and the accompanying deflation and overcapacity are going to drive the economy and financial markets in 2010. We have said this repeatedly that this recession is really a depression because the [post-WW II] recessions were merely small backward steps in an inventory cycle but in the context of expanding credit. Whereas now, we are in a prolonged period of credit contraction, especially as it relates to households and small businesses.[1]

Rosenberg highlighted asset deflation and credit contraction, imploding "the largest balance sheet in the world—the US household sector" in the amount of "an epic $12 trillion of lost net worth, a degree of trauma we have never seen before," despite the tenuous recovery and equity market rally, based more on hope and manipulation than reality.

As a result, consumer spending has been far from robust. "Frugality is the new fashion and likely to stay that way for years," highlighting a secular shift toward prudence and conservatism because households are traumatized, tapped out, and mindful of a bleak outlook, especially in a weak job market with real unemployment topping 20%, not the fake Labor Department reports based on manipulated data.

On March 5, 2011, economist Paul Craig Roberts' article headlined, "More Jobs Mirage,"[2] commenting on the fraudulent March employment report. Claiming 192,000 new jobs were created in February, he wrote, "is just more smoke and mirrors."

In fact, there were no jobs created; economist John Williams[3] (using 1980 methodology) said about 38,000 were lost, and explained as follows: the Bureau of Labor Statistics (BLS) fraudulent "birth-death model" estimates net non-reported jobs from new businesses minus losses from others no longer operating. During expansions, the model works because start-ups exceed shut-downs. It doesn't work in recessions. Yet the BLS assumes employees from non-operating companies are still there. In addition, BLS adds 30,000 jobs monthly whether or not new companies exist.

"Williams estimates the 'death' side [calculation] reduce[s] employment by about 200,000 per month, and the 'birth' side [is] stillborn." As a result, BLS overestimated February 2011 job creation by 230,000. "The benchmark revisions of payroll jobs bear" him out, showing "a reduction of previously reported employment gains of about 2 million jobs."[4]

Moreover, despite a decade of population growth, about nine million fewer Americans are now employed, a shocking indictment of a broken economy, bolstered by fake BLS reports. "Some 'New Economy,' " noted Roberts. "If only we could have the old one back."

It's not in sight and won't likely be for the foreseeable future.

Economic Turmoil in 2011

Wall Street predicts blue skies. Economic recovery will continue. Stocks will deliver double-digit gains. On January 14, 2011, the *Wall Street Journal*'s Economic Forecast Survey headlined, "Economists Optimistic on Growth,"[5] expecting in 2011:

- 3.3% GDP growth;

- unemployment declining to 8.8%;

- inflation contained at 1.9%;

- crude oil at around $90 a barrel;

- improved housing starts in a depressed market;

- on average, 180,000 monthly jobs created;

- no Fed interest rate hike until 2012 at the earliest;

- continued QE II buying of $600 - $900 billion in government bonds; and

- an overall upbeat sentiment for economic recovery and growth.

Others disagree, including long-time insider/market analyst Bob Chapman, calling current economic policy destabilizing enough to have profound future social costs. Sometime in 2011, he says, conditions are "going to be nasty. The handwriting is on the wall." But no one's listening.

On January 20, the *Financial Times* headlined, "US States Face a Fiscal Crunch," saying:

> Undue budget tightening will jeopardize recovery whether applied at the federal level or lower down....The squeeze is not upon them; the federal stimulus is fading away, and the gimmicks are all used up. For state finances, the year of reckoning has arrived, and the timing could hardly be worse.

Global European Anticipation Bulletin (GEAB) analysts are also expecting hard times. On January 16, 2011, their new economic assessment headlined, "Systemic global crisis—2011: The ruthless year, at the crossroads of three roads of global chaos," predictied "entry into the terminal phase of the world before the crisis."

Since 2008, policies undertaken hid economic deterioration instead of resolving it. The present year "will mark the crucial moment when... palliative measures" no longer work, and "the consequences of systemic dislocation...dramatically surge to the forefront."

In 2011, "violent shocks....will explode the faulty safety devices put in place since 2008" and will erode the "pillars" on which the "Dollar Wall" rested for decades until gold no longer backed it. Overall, 2011 will be chaotic. All bets are off. "The crisis ball rolls and everyone holds their breath so it doesn't fall" squarely on them.

Soaring food, energy and other commodity prices will continue. Inflation will rise. It's higher than reported. Tunisia is instructive. Impacted by high food and energy prices as well as unemployment, American and other "godfathers" couldn't prevent street protests collapsing a friendly regime, now struggling to reinvent itself, unsuccessfully so far.

America's leadership is eroding. Europe is weak, and BRIC countries (Brazil, Russia, India and China) are not ready to control the global economy and so can only "quietly undermine what remains of the foundations of pre-crisis order."

Fragility defines 2011 with many nations "on the verge of socio-economic break-up," especially America and Europe where real unemployment and poverty are rising, social benefits are disappearing, and angry people are beginning to react. The incendiary mix "that's the making of political time bombs."

History often signals warnings "before sweeping away the past." It came in 2008, with 2011 to "do the sweeping." Only nations that can "adapt to the new conditions" will weather them. "[F]or the others, chaos is at the end of the road."[6]

On March 17, 2011, LEAP analysts headlined, "Get ready for the meltdown of the US Treasury Bond market," saying because of Middle East uprisings and Japan's nuclear disaster, expect Gulf states and Tokyo to halt US Treasury purchases. In fact, Japan's crisis will force asset repatriations needed "to finance the enormous cost of stabilization, reconstruction, and revival of [its] economy."[7]

Moreover, China's growing reluctance to buy US debt will further pressure the market. In addition, it's "highly significant that PIMCO, the world's largest bond fund manager, decided at the end of February 2011, to liquidate" US Treasuries, judging them too risky to hold. Along with unstable and weakening global economies, LEAP analysts believe US Treasuries "will be the first major collateral casualty" of systemic instability, likely in Q 3 or 4, 2011.

Trends forecaster Gerald Celente says 2011 will be a "wake-up call [for] how grave economic conditions have become" because of ineffective, self-serving, counterproductive solutions. As a result, he sees "crack-up" ahead based on reliable indicators like unemployment, housing, currencies and sovereign debt problems, "all border[ing]]between crisis and disaster."[8]

Teetering economies will collapse. Currency wars will continue. Trade barriers will be erected. Economic unions will splinter, and "the onset of the 'Greatest Depression' [will be] recognized by everyone." As governments "extract funds to meet fiscal obligations," working populations will be hurt most, and they'll react publicly, including by hardship-driven crimes, whatever it takes to survive. A "war on crime" will follow, with everyone guilty unless proved innocent.

"The closer we get to 2012, the louder the calls will be that the 'End is Near!'" For many, it'll feel that way because of harder than ever hard times.

Economist Michael Hudson's January 18, 2011 article headlined, "The Specter Haunting Europe: Debt Defaults, Austerity, and Death of the 'Social Europe' Model,"[9] saying:

> EU policy seems to be for wage earners and pension savers to bail out banks for their legacy of bad mortgages and other loans that cannot be paid—except by plunging their economies into poverty.

If wages decline, high debt burdens "become even heavier....Aside from the misery and human tragedies that will multiply in [their] wake, fiscal and wage austerity is economically self-destructive."

Eventually demand is crushed, turning recessions into depressions. Instead of creditors getting hurt, however, imposed "post-modern neoserfdom....threatens to return Europe to its pre-modern state." Working Americans face the same plight under bipartisan planned austerity, heading a once prosperous country toward third world status, complete with militarized enforcement once anger erupts.

It's the debt and bad government policy, stupid—a pig no amount of lipstick can hide—and when it explodes, reverberations will be felt more than ever globally. It's coming, but no one knows when, despite most rosy forecasts.

The tougher things become, the more deceptive MSM assessments get, saying the crisis has passed. Claiming better economic times ahead doesn't wash in the face of a global debt crisis which is accelerating, not abating. Strapped US states are teetering on insolvency, failing to contain their own debt burdens through draconian austerity budgets on the backs of American workers, people least able to cope.

Obama's solution is less, not more, regulation. His January 18 Executive Order (EO) headlined, "Improving Regulation and Regulatory Review" proposed "Flexible Approaches," requiring review of all existing regulations to ease them for powerful corporate interests. It requires federal agencies to "adopt [them] only upon a reasoned determination that" benefits justify costs.

After decades of regulatory implosion, Obama plans more, no matter how destructive freewheeling freedom became, especially after the global economic crisis took hold, heading us for worse hard times, not a resolution lifting all boats.

US States in Crisis

Faced with huge budget deficits, US states, with few exceptions, are cutting jobs, wages and benefits as well as raising taxes at the worst time when stimulus is needed. Since 2008, California, New York, Michigan and others have been on the brink or getting there, worse off now because the measures taken have been counterproductive.

Illinois is a case in point, with the nation's worst budget crisis per capita. Yet the crisis has been confronted the wrong way by raising taxes, making big cuts in health care (including Medicaid), education and other social services. In addition, thousands of state workers were laid off, pay and benefits cuts were imposed for others, and more is planned going forward.

Collectively in FY 2011, state governments face about a $175 billion deficit, besides major shortfalls in large and small cities. In fact, according to Nick Johnson of the Center on Budget and Policy Priorities, this year "will actually be the most difficult budget year for states ever,"[10] and 2012 may be as or more challenging.

Moreover, unlike 2010, little or no federal aid is planned with Washington in discretionary spending austerity mode. It means states and working Americans will largely be on their own to cope.

On January 5, New York Governor Andrew Cuomo's State of the State address suggests what's coming nationwide. Facing a projected $9 billion deficit, he outlined proposed draconian cuts in education, health care, and state payrolls, including pay and benefits, saying "New York spends too much money." So to curb it, he also wants a 20% reduction in state agencies, authorities and commissions, while pledging to keep New York "business friendly," meaning workers will feel pain, not fat cats.

Accordingly, he announced no tax increase for the wealthy and will let a so-called temporary "millionaire's tax" surcharge on $200,000 a year or more earners expire, depriving the state of $1 billion annually.

Illinois in Deep Crisis

The University of Illinois' Institute of Government & Public Affairs (IGPA) headlined a recent report, "Illinois Budget Woes: Titanic and Sinking,"[11] stating that state problems aren't new, but lawmakers haven't "developed a strategy for resolving the situation and it is rapidly growing worse." Moreover, IGPA analysts say:

> the state's fiscal disaster is even worse than commonly
> believed, will take years or even decades to remedy and
> can be fixed only by large and fundamental changes in
> both spending and tax policies....

With spending exceeding revenues, and obligations not postponed, unpaid bills are growing "at a frightening rate. For instance, IGPA's Fiscal Futures Model indicates [they] could reach $40 billion by July 1, 2013, with an associated delay in paying those bills of more than five years."

Besides its $13 billion deficit and $6 billion in unpaid bills, its pension fund is about $130 billion in the red—a red flag indicating that state workers may lose out altogether on their promised retirement savings. Overall, achieving a balanced 2012 budget requires one or a combination of three alternatives:

- enormous increases in personal and corporate taxes to 7.1% and 11.3% respectively;

- raising the current 6.25% sales tax to 13.5%, and/or

- cutting spending across the board by 26%, exclusive of debt service, pensions and transportation.

Moreover, IGPA concluded that state fiscal problems "are so enormous that no single tactic will be enough to balance the budget....We start so out of balance that even an absolute freeze on all spending will not achieve balance [over] a 10-year time horizon. Bringing Illinois to fiscal solvency will require state government to implement multiple and massive policy changes. If nothing is done soon, [Illinois] faces a very bleak future."

In fact, working households already do, as they may feel pain for decades, including higher (private and public) unemployment or underemployment because of disastrous federal and state policies.

Illinois State Legislature Acts

On January 12, 2011, *Chicago Tribune* writers Ray Long and Monique Garcia headlined, "[Gov.] Quinn congratulated Democrats on income tax increase," saying that with no Republican support, House and Senate Democrats (on the last legislative day before newly elected lawmakers take over) passed a major income tax increase, "rais[ing] the personal [rate] by 67 percent and the business [rate] by 46 percent."

As a result, the personal tax rate rose from 3% to 5%, then will drop to 3.75% in 2015 and 3.25% in 2025 unless the budget crisis remains dire enough to require further tax increases, not cuts—a distinct possibility.

Corporate rates rose from 4.8% to 7% until 2015, then will drop to 5.25% in 2015 and 4.8% in 2025, depending on budget priorities and whether Republicans or Democrats are in charge.

Tax changes were effective retroactive to January 1, 2011 and will raise an estimated $6.5 billion in 12 months, way short of what's needed, and estimates have a way of not being met. In addition, the new law plans:

> to limit spending in each of the next four budget years—$36.8 billion in FY 2012, $37.5 billion in FY 2013, $38.3 billion in 2014 and $39 billion in 2015. The state's auditor general would determine if lawmakers and the governor exceed those spending limits. [If so], the higher income tax rates would revert to current levels.

Running for reelection, Quinn campaigned on a smaller income tax increase—a promise made and broken the way Washington does repeatedly, including Obama who broke every major pledge he made, literally thumbing his nose at constituents by governing irresponsibly. Illinois is run the same way under Democrats or Republicans. That's why the state is insolvent.

In January 2010, Crain's *Chicago Business* reported:

Illinois appears to meet classic definitions of insolvency: Its liabilities far exceed its assets, and it's not generating enough cash to pay its bills.

According to IGPA senior fellow Jim Nowlan, Illinois is "close to de facto bankruptcy, if not de jure bankruptcy."

Laurence Msall, Civic Federation president, a Chicago fiscal watchdog agreed, saying:

We would like all the stakeholders of Illinois to recognize how close the state is to bankruptcy or insolvency.

According to legal experts, federal bankruptcy code protections apply only to cities and counties, not states. Nonetheless, even new tax revenues may not satisfy obligations, making some form of fiscal collapse inevitable. Moreover, as unpaid bills accumulate, venders may stop dealing with the state and investors won't buy Illinois bonds.

According to University of Illinois/Chicago Economics Professor David Merriman, "The crisis will come when you see state institutions shutting down because they can't pay their employees" or bills.

Rising pension payments are another factor pushing Illinois over the edge. *Crain's Chicago Business* report warned that:

the radical cost-cutting and huge tax increases necessary to pay all [its] deferred costs from the past would become so large that many businesses and individuals would be driven out of Illinois, thereby magnifying the vicious cycle of contracting state services, increasing taxes, and loss of the state's tax base.[12]

Although Illinois' Constitution protects vested pension benefits, paying them depends on resources to do it. According to the Civic Federation, evidence suggests that:

a judge could find the state insolvent. [If so] under the classical cash-flow definition of insolvency, which is 'the inability to pay debts as they come due,' it is not only the pension rights of non-vested employees that will be in jeopardy. All the obligations of the state, whether vested or not, will be competing for funding with the other essential responsibilities of state government. Even vested pension rights are jeopardized when a government is [declared] insolvent."[13]

Outlook in 2011

What's true for Illinois affects most other states facing the most dire times since the Great Depression. Nonetheless, the Obama administration and 112th Congress plan no federal state bailouts ahead. Moreover, Fed chairman Bernanke said "We have no expectation or intention to get involved in state and local finance," and according to Rep. Paul Ryan (R. WI): "If we bail out one state, then all of the debt of all of the states are almost explicitly on the books of the federal government," which is already drowning in its own.

Yet the combined shortfall of all states equals a tiny fraction of all defense spending (including supplemental add-ons, black budgets, debt service, veterans benefits, and other expenses). Moreover, it's one-fifth of the initial $700 billion TARP bank bailout, and a miniscule percent of the estimated $13 trillion+ given rogue banksters.

Nonetheless, Washington's message to states and American workers apparently is "Let 'em eat cake." Whether or not Marie Antoinette actually said it, France's 1789-1799 revolution was very real, delivering guillotine justice, not promised "Liberté, Egalité, et Fraternité."

Endnotes

1   David Rosenberg, "David Rosenberg's Outlook For 2010," *Business Insider*, December 10, 2009, available at <http://www.businessinsider.com/henry-blodget-david-rosenbergs-outlook-for-2010-2009-12>

2   Paul Craig Roberts, "More Jobs Mirage" March 4, 2011, available at *globalresearch.ca* <http://globalresearch.ca/index.php?context=va&aid=23541>

3   See *John Williams' Shadow Government Statistics: Analysis Behind and Beyond Government Economic Reporting*, <http://www.shadowstats.com>

4   Paul Craig Roberts, supra note 2.

5   Phil Izzo, "Economists Optimistic on Growth", *Wall Street Journal*, January 14, 2011, available at < http://online.wsj.com/article/SB10001424052748704307404576079870784741108.html>

6   GEAB, "The Systemic Global Economic Crisis: At the Crossroads of Three Roads of Global Chaos", *Globalresearch.ca*, January 19, 2011, available at <http://globalresearch.ca/index.php?context=va&aid=22862>

7   LEAP, "Global systemic crisis: Second half of 2011—Get ready for the meltdown of the US Treasury Bond market" Public announcement GEAB N°53 (March 17, 2011), available at <http://www.leap2020.eu/Global-systemic-crisis-Second-half-of-2011-Get-ready-for-the-meltdown-of-the-US-Treasury-Bond-market_a6091.html>

8   Gerald Celente, Wake Up Call Documentary, *Trends & Forecasts*, January 1, 2011, available at <http://geraldcelentechannel.blogspot.com/2011/01/wake-up-call-new-world-order.html>

9   Available at <http://globalresearch.ca/index.php?context=va&aid=22846>

10   Tami Luhby, "Budget Axe Falls on New York," *CNN.com*, January 19, 2010, at <http://money.cnn.com/2010/01/19/news/economy/New_York_budget_deficit/index.htm>

11   Available at <http://igpa.uillinois.edu/IR11/Titanic-and-sinking/>

12   Crain's *Chicago Business* report, *Illinois enters a state of insolvency*, January 18, 2010.

13   Id.

9

MANIPULATION
HOW MARKETS REALLY WORK

Wall Street claims markets move randomly, reflecting the collective wisdom of investors. The truth is quite opposite. The government's visible hand and insiders control them, manipulating them up or down for profit—all of them, including stocks, bonds, commodities and currencies. The public is none the wiser.

It's brazen financial fraud—what former high-level Wall Street insider/former Assistant HUD Secretary Catherine Austin Fitts[1] calls "pump and dump," defined as "artificially inflating the price of a stock or other security through promotion, in order to sell at the inflated price," then profit more on the downside by short-selling. "This practice is illegal under securities law, yet it is particularly common," and in today's volatile markets occurs daily to one degree or other.

Why? Because the profits are enormous, in good and bad times, and when carried to extremes, Fitts calls it "pump[ing] and dump[ing] of the entire American economy," duping the public, fleecing trillions from them, and it's more than just "a process designed to wipe out the middle class. This is genocide [by other means]—a much more subtle and lethal version than ever before perpetrated by the scoundrels of our history texts."[2]

Much more, in fact, goes on, amounting to a "financial coup d'etat, including fraudulent housing [and other bubbles], pump and dump schemes, naked short selling, precious metals price suppression [or acceleration], and active intervention in the markets by the government and central bank" along with insiders.

It's a government/business cabal for enormous profits through legislation, contracts, regulation (or lack thereof), financing, subsidies, and massive amounts of handouts, much of it secret. More still overall by rigging the game for powerful insiders, while at the same time harming the public so cleverly that few know what's happening or why. Media touts won't explain, falsely citing bogus reasons, good or bad.

Market Rigging Mechanisms—The Plunge Protection Team

On March 18, 1989, Ronald Reagan's Executive Order 12631 created the Working Group on Financial Markets (WGFM), commonly called the Plunge Protection Team (PPT). It consisted of the following officials or their designees:

- the President;

- the Treasury Secretary as chairman;

- the Fed chairman;

- the SEC chairman; and

- the Commodity Futures Trading Commission chairman.

Under Sec. 2, its "Purposes and Functions" were stated as follows:

> (2) Recognizing the goals of enhancing the integrity, efficiency, orderliness, and competitiveness of our Nation's financial markets and maintaining investor confidence, the Working Group shall identify and consider:
>
> > (1) the major issues raised by the numerous studies on the events [pertaining to the] October 19, 1987 [market crash and consider] recommendations that have the potential to achieve the goals noted above; and
> >
> > (2)...governmental [and other] actions under existing laws and regulations... that are appropriate to carry out these recommendations.

In August 2005, Canada-based Sprott Asset Management (SAM) principals John Embry and Andrew Hepburn issued a report titled "Move Over, Adam Smith—The Visible Hand of Uncle Sam"[3] on the US government's "surreptitious" market interventions to prevent "destabilizing stock market declines. Comprising key government agencies, stock exchanges and large Wall Street firms," this group "is significant because the government has never admitted to private-sector membership in the Working Group," nor is it hinting that manipulation works both ways—to stop *and to create* panic.

> Current mythology holds that [equity] prices rise and
> fall on the basis of market forces alone. Such sentiments
> appear to be seriously mistaken...And as official rhetoric
> continues to toe the free market line, manipulation
> has become increasingly apparent...with the active
> participation of selected investment banks and brokerage
> houses [the Wall Street giants].[4]

In 2004, Texas Hedge Report principals Steven McIntyre and Todd
Stein said "[a]lmost every floor trader on the NYSE, NYMEX, CBOT and CME
will admit to having seen the PPT in action in one form or another over the
years"[5]—violating the traditional notion that markets move randomly and
reflect popular sentiment.

Worse still, according to Embry and Hepburn, "the government's
unwillingness to disclose its activities has rendered it very difficult to have a
debate on the merits of such a policy," if there are any.

Further, "virtually no one ever mentions government intervention
publicly...Our primary concern is that what apparently started as a stopgap
measure may have morphed into a serious moral hazard situation."

Worst of all, if government and Wall Street collude to pump and
dump markets, individuals and small investment firms can get trampled,
and that's exactly what happened in 2008 and early 2009, with much more
coming as the greatest economic crisis since the Great Depression plays out
over many more months, maybe years.

That said, the PPT might more aptly be called the PPDT—The Plunge
Protection/Destruction Team, depending on which way it moves markets at
any time. Investors beware.

Manipulating markets is commonplace and as old as investing.
Only the tools get more sophisticated and the amounts greater. In her book,
Morgan: American Financier,[6] Jean Strouse explained his role in the Panic of
1907, the result of stock market and real estate speculation that caused a
market crash, bank runs, and hysteria. To restore confidence, JP Morgan and
the Treasury Secretary organized a group of financiers to transfer funds to
troubled banks and buy stocks. At the time, rumors were rampant that they
orchestrated the panic for speculative profits and to advance their main goals:

- the 1908 National Monetary Commission to stabilize financial
  markets—a precursor to the Federal Reserve; and

- the 1910 Jekyll Island meeting where powerful financial figures met
  in secret for nine days and created the private banking cartel Federal
  Reserve System, later congressionally established on December 23,
  1913 and signed into law by Woodrow Wilson.

Morgan died early that year but profited hugely from the 1907 Panic. It let him expand his steel empire by buying the Tennessee Coal and Iron Company for about $45 million, an asset thought to be worth around $700 million. Today, similar schemes are more common than ever in the wake of the global economic crisis, letting bankers and other corporate predators buy assets cheap with bailout or borrowed cash. Aided by PPT market rigging, it's simpler than ever.

Wharton Professor Itay Goldstein and Said Business School and Lincoln College, Oxford University Professor Alexander Guembel discussed price manipulation in their paper titled "Manipulation and the Allocational Role of Prices." They showed how traders affect prices on the downside through "bear raids," concluding:

> We basically describe a theory of how bear raid
> manipulation works...What we show here is that by selling
> [a stock or more effectively short-selling it], you have a
> real effect on the firm. The connection with real value is
> the new thing...This is the crucial element...[7]

but they claim the process only works on the downside, not driving shares up.

In fact, high-volume program trading, analyst recommendations, positive or negative media reports, and other devices do it both ways.

Also key: a company's stock price and true worth can be highly divergent. In other words, healthy or sick firms may be way over- or under-valued depending on market and economic conditions and how manipulative traders wish to price them, short or longer term.

The idea that equity prices reflect true value or that markets move randomly (up or down) is nonsense. They never have and more than ever, don't now.

The Exchange Stabilization Fund (ESF)

The 1934 Gold Reserve Act created the US Treasury's ESF. Section 7 of the 1944 Bretton Woods Agreements made its operations permanent. As originally established, the Treasury ran the Fund outside of congressional oversight "to keep sharp swings in the dollar's exchange rate from [disrupting] financial markets" through manipulation. Its operations now include stabilizing foreign currencies, extending credit lines to foreign governments, and in September 2008, guaranteeing money market funds against losses for up to $50 billion.

In 1995, the Clinton administration used the fund to provide Mexico a $20 billion credit line to stabilize the peso at a time of economic crisis, and earlier administrations extended loans or credit lines to China, Brazil, Ecuador, Iceland and Liberia. The Treasury's website also states that:

> By law, the Secretary has considerable discretion in the use of ESF resources. The legal basis of the ESF is the Gold Reserve Act of 1934. As amended in the late 1970s...the Secretary [per] approval of the President, may deal in gold, foreign exchange, and other instruments of credit and securities.

In other words, ESF is a slush fund for whatever purposes the Treasury wishes, including ones it may not wish to disclose, such as manipulating markets, directing funds to the IMF and providing them to borrowers with strings attached, as the Treasury's site explains:

> ...Treasury has often linked the availability of ESF financing to a borrower's use of the credit facilities of the IMF, both to support the IMF's role and to strengthen assurances that there will be timely repayment of ESF financing.

The Counterparty Risk Management Policy Group (CRMPG)

Established in 1999 in the wake of the Long Term Capital Management (LTCM) crisis, it manipulates markets to benefit Wall Street giants and high-level insiders. According to one account, it was to curb future crises by:

- letting giant financial institutions collude through large-scale program trading to move markets up or down as they wish;

- bailing out its members in financial trouble; and

- manipulating markets short or longer term with government approval at the expense of small investors who were none the wiser and often getting trampled.

In August 2008, CRMPG III issued a report titled "Containing Systemic Risk: The Road to Reform."[8] It was deceptive on its face in stating that CRMPG "was designed to focus its primary attention on the steps that must be taken by the private sector to reduce the frequency and/or severity of future financial shocks while recognizing that such future shocks are inevitable, in part because it is literally impossible to anticipate the specific timing and triggers of such events."

In fact, the "private sector" creates "financial shocks" to open markets, remove competition, and consolidate for greater power by buying damaged assets cheap. Financial history has numerous examples of preying on the weak, crushing competition, socializing risks, privatizing profits, and redistributing wealth upward to a financial oligarchy, creating tollbooth economies in debt bondage, and overall getting a free lunch at the public's expense.

CRMPG explains financial excesses and crises this way:

> At the end of the day, [their] root cause...on both the upside and the downside of the cycle is collective human behavior: unbridled optimism on the upside and fear on the downside, all in a setting in which it is literally impossible to anticipate when optimism gives rise to fear or fear gives rise to optimism...
>
> What is needed, therefore, is a form of private initiative that will complement official oversight in encouraging industry-wide practices that will help mitigate systemic risk. The recommendations of the Report have been framed with that objective in mind.

In other words, let foxes guard the henhouse to keep inventing new ways to extract gains (a free lunch) in increasingly larger amounts—"in the interest of helping to contain systemic risk factors and promote greater stability."

Or as Orwell might have said: instability is stability, creating systemic risk is containing it, sloping playing fields are level ones, extracting the greatest profit is sharing it, and what benefits the few helps everyone.

In fact, market collapses can be very profitable. Security and Exchange Commission (SEC) regulators created an environment supporting speculation through futures, options, index funds, derivative securities, and short-selling, etc.

As a result, with foreknowledge (inside information), money can be made in either up or down markets, creating golden opportunities for powerful speculators, using enormous amounts of leveraged funds, to capitalize.

As a result, concentrated wealth and financial power resulting from market manipulation is unprecedented with small investors' savings, IRAs, pensions, 401ks, and futures being decimated by it.

Forewarned is forearmed.

Endnotes

1   Fitts is editor of the financial website, Solari, at http://solari.com.

2   Catherine Austin Fitts, "Why I Wrote This Story", available at <http://dunwalke.com/introduction.htm>

3   John Embry and Andrew Hepburn, "Move Over Adam Smith: The Visible Hand of

Uncle Sam", August, 2005. Available at <http://www.sprott.com/Docs/SpecialReports/08_2005_TheVisibleHand.pdf>

4   Id.

5   Steven McIntyre and Todd Stein, "Gold Manipulation is a Blessing," *The Texas Hedge Report* (December 10, 2004): http://www.safehaven.com/showarticle. cfm?id=2318&pv=1. Cited in Embry and Hepburn, supra note 3.

6   Jeane Strouse, *Morgan: American Financier*, Random House, 1999.

7   Itay Goldstein and Alexander Guembel, "Manipulation and the Allocational Role of Prices", *Review of Economic Studies,* Vol. 75, No. 1, pp. 133-164, January 2008.

8   Available at <http://www.crmpolicygroup.org/docs/CRMPG-III.pdf>

10

GOLDMAN SACHS
MASTER OF THE UNIVERSE

"Master of the Universe" applies to all Wall Street giants, but to none like Goldman, the Grand Master. Like the fabled comic book Superman hero, it's:

- faster than its competitors, thanks to its proprietary software ability to front run markets (illegal, but no matter);

- more powerful than the government it controls; and

- able to leap past competitors, given its special status.

Founded in 1869, GS calls itself "a leading global investment banking, securities and investment management firm that provides a wide range of services worldwide."

Since going public in 1999, the same year Glass-Steagall ended, letting banks, insurers and securities companies combine, GS became a giant hedge fund trading against the advice given clients with the full faith and blessing of Washington—the same thing other Street giants do and profit from handsomely.

In his April 17, 2010 article headlined, "Goldman Sachs Vampire Squid Gets Handcuffed," L. Randall Wray noted SEC laxity for years, "managing to sleep through every bubble and bust in recent memory," then saying Goldman acts above the law "since it took over Washington during the Clinton years." Their criminal behavior is nothing new. It's their business model, the reason it's been immersed in nearly all financial scandals since the 19th century.

John Kenneth Galbraith's famous 1954 book, *The Great Crash*, had a chapter titled "In Goldman We Trust" on its contribution to the Great Depression through risky investment trusts (an early mutual fund cum Ponzi scheme) sold to unwary buyers.

Goldman and others fueled speculative fever in shares, reaping highly leveraged capital gains with other people's money. They were fraudulent pyramid schemes, like Charles Ponzi/Bernie Madoff scams. Then and today, they collapsed, the way they always do when insiders pull the plug, at the same time cashing out to let unwary customers take the pain.

At the end of his Goldman chapter, Galbraith recounted this exchange after the crash before a Senate committee:

Senator Couzens: Did Goldman, Sachs and Company organize the Goldman Sachs Trading Corporation [to sell junk trusts to unwary buyers]?

Mr. Sachs: Yes, sir.

Senator Couzens: And it sold its stock to the public?

Mr. Sachs: A portion of it. The firm invested originally in 10 per cent of the entire issue for the sum of $10,000,000.

Senator Couzens: And the other 90 per cent was sold to the public?

Mr. Sachs: Yes, sir.

Senator Couzens: At what price?

Mr. Sachs: At 104. That is the old stock....the stock was split two for one.

Senator Couzens: And what is the price of the stock now?

Mr. Sachs: Approximately 1 and 3/4.

In other words, it was practically worthless, losing over 98% of its value. GS scammed investors, with the unlucky ones losing their shirt. For some, perhaps everything.

Unwary buyers then and now always lose out, not knowing that betting against Goldman assures getting fleeced. Yet even sophisticated lambs volunteer to be slaughtered, thinking they're as smart, will get out in time, then learning otherwise and discovering Goldman cheats all clients, even nations like Greece by hiding its debt and shorting it. Around a dozen US states as well, including California, are treated the same way.

Wall Street's culture encourages fraud, rewarding it handsomely practically risk-free. The price for getting caught usually amounts to fines too small to matter, chump change compared to the fortunes stolen.

Will this or future times be different? No matter the cost to others, like Enron and the Savings and Loan crooks? Don't ever bet against Goldman, especially given the SEC's shoddy crime fighting record, picking off small fry but barely slowing big ones, at most, imposing hand slaps too meager to matter. More on SEC non-enforcement below.

So what to make of *New York Times* writers Louise Story and Gretchen Morgenson's April 16, 2010 article, headlined, "SEC Accuses Goldman of Fraud in Housing Deal"?

The SEC civil, not criminal, suit named Fabrice Tourre, "the fabulous Fab," (GS's 31-year old VP involved in creating junk investments), charging fraud. GS, in turn, called the accusations "completely unfounded in law and fact [and would] vigorously contest them and defend the firm and its reputation." Indeed so, with all the legal talent billions in ready assets can buy, and no shortage of top tort attorneys willing to take it.

Other suits may follow, but was Goldman punished? Hardly. By mid-year, it settled for $550 million, case closed, the equivalent of four 2009 revenue days. For a firm large as Goldman, it hardly mattered, especially as no executive was fined or jailed. Moreover, GS renewed its license to steal, but the headlines didn't explain. Only its scammed customers know the truth.

SEC Charges Now Resolved

On April 16, 2010, the SEC:

> charged Goldman, Sachs & Co. and one of its vice presidents for defrauding investors by misstating and omitting key facts about a financial product tied to subprime mortgages as the US housing market was beginning to falter.

The allegations were:

> that Goldman Sachs structured and marketed a synthetic collateralized debt obligation (CDO) that hinged on the performance of subprime residential mortgage-backed securities (RMBS). Goldman Sachs failed to disclose to investors vital information about the CDO, in particular the role that a major hedge fund played in the portfolio selection process and the role that the hedge fund (Paulson

& Co.) played in the portfolio selection process and the fact that the hedge fund had taken a short position against the CDO"—junk assets its president, John Paulson, made $4 billion on in 2007 by correctly betting on the housing collapse he and GS helped initiate.

The SEC's complaint charges Goldman Sachs and Tourre with violations of Section 17(a) of the Securities Act of 1933, Section 10(b) of the Securities Exchange Act of 1934, and Exchange Act Rule 10b-5. The Commission seeks injunctive relief, disgorgement of profits, prejudgment interest, and financial penalties.[1]

Fabrice Tourre was "principally responsible" for the fraud and sent an email before they were sold saying, "the whole building is about to collapse anytime now," calling himself the "[o]nly potential survivor, the fabulous Fab....standing in the middle of all these complex, highly leveraged, exotic trades he created without necessarily understanding all of the implications of those 'monstrosities!!!'"[2]

According to the SEC, he wasn't alone, as senior GS executives signed off on them. Likely but unnamed, they included CEO Lloyd Blankfein—profiled on November 8, 2009 in the *London Sunday Times* saying "I'm doing 'God's work,' " the height of audacity matching the firm's history of criminality and getting away with it.

In fact, executives up to and including Blankfein took an active role in overseeing GS's mortgage unit as financial tremors hit America's housing market. At the same time, company officials shorted the market while advising clients to buy. Around 99% of the mortgage securities sold went sour. Investors at first were unaware they'd been scammed. It's how GS always operates.

Definition of Fraud

Black's Law Dictionary, 5th edition, 1979 defines fraud as follows:

All multifarious means which human ingenuity can devise, and which are resorted to by one individual to get an advantage over another by false suggestions or suppression of the truth. It includes all surprises, tricks, cunning or dissembling, and any unfair way which another is cheated.

The legal dictionary, *thefreedictionary.com,* calls it:

A false representation of a matter of fact—whether by words or by conduct, by false or misleading allegations, or by concealment of what should have been disclosed—that deceives and is intended to deceive another so that the individual will act upon it to her or his legal injury.

Criminal and civil frauds differ in the level of proof required. The former needs a "preponderance of evidence." The latter must prove intent and be "beyond a reasonable doubt."

Unsurprisingly, GS settled for pennies on the dollar, given the SEC's deplorable history of being more facilitator than regulator. It's now run Mary Schapiro, a high level industry insider, through a revolving door into her position before returning to another top spot.

Before being appointed, she was CEO of the Financial Industry Regulatory Authority (FINRA), served as president of NASD Regulation (National Association of Securities Dealers), then was NASD's chairman and CEO. Earlier she was an SEC commissioner, and in 2008, George Bush appointed her to the newly established President's Advisory Council on Financial Literacy, focusing on economic empowerment issues.

She was also chairperson of the IOSCO SRO Consultative Committee under Bush, another body supposedly "promot[ing] high standards of regulation in order to maintain just, efficient and sound markets," the same ones manipulated to collapse, while the SEC and other watchdogs stayed silent and watched.

Despite plenty of culpability to go around among major banks and their complicit hedge fund and other trading partners, Karl Denninger explained part of the prosecutorial problem besides SEC laxity:

The real problem is with these so-called 'complex securities' that are in fact nothing more than a gambling contract designed and constructed in such a fashion as to make proper due diligence impossible. Some of these synthetics had literally 100,000 pages of referenced documentation related to them—how can anyone reasonably expect to read and understand that sort of paperwork?

Even worse, they're "abusive [because] someone believes that the reference security or securities in question will decline...."

In other words, they're structured to fail—clear evidence of criminal intent by companies and complicit employees. But will SEC officials ever charge it? Will the Justice Department pursue RICO violations involving the largest financial fraud in history with plenty of guilt to go around? They didn't, haven't, and won't, except perhaps against some low-level sacrificial lambs, falling on their swords to absolve higher-ups, those most responsible.

The Power of Goldman in Government, Central Banking and International Financial Institutions

On October 17, 2008, *New York Times* writers Julie Creswell and Ben White's article headlined, "The Guys from 'Government Sachs,' " showing how embedded they are in Washington—so much so that competitors call them "Government Sachs."

Long regarded as Wall Street's savviest firm, "The power and influence that Goldman wields at the nexus of politics and finance is no accident." It has a history and culture of "encouraging its partners to take leadership roles in public service," for the obvious benefit to the firm.

Among insiders, it's widely acknowledged that "no matter how much money you pile up, you are not a true Goldman star until you make your mark in the political sphere." According to some, it's a conflict of interest, since the decisions they can make then directly benefit the firm.

Former Treasury Secretary Henry Paulson was appointed because of Joshua B. Bolten, former GS alum and GW Bush chief of staff. "And if there is one thing Goldman has, it is an imposing army of top-of-their-class, up-before-dawn uber-achievers."

Other Paulson Treasury stalwarts included:

- Neel Kashkari, who originally ran a $700 billion fund buying toxic assets before becoming Interim Assistant Treasury Secretary for Financial Stability under Paulson, his "right-hand man," according to *The Times*, playing a major role in selling Bear Stearns to JP Morgan;

- Dan Jester, former GS strategic officer involved in 2008 Treasury initiatives, especially the Fannie and Freddie takeovers and bailing out his former employer;

- Steve Shafran, formerly a GS Asian executive involved in Treasury's guarantee of money market funds among other activities;

- Kendrick Wilson III, "a seasoned adviser to chief executives of the nation's biggest banks;" unpaid, he worked on apprising them of possible Treasury plans to get their reaction;

- Edward Forst, a former Paulson adviser on setting up the bailout fund, who then returned to his position as Harvard executive vice president;

- Robert K. Steel, Goldman's former vice chairman, hired to shore up Fannie and Freddie.

Other prominent alumni include:

- Robert Rubin, former co-chairman and Treasury Secretary;

- John Corzine, former CEO and chairman, US senator and New Jersey governor;

- Robert Zoellick, former managing director, Deputy Secretary of State and US Trade Representative, and current World Bank president;

- Jeffrey Reuben III, former European managing partner and Under Secretary of State;

- Mark Patterson, former Goldman lobbyist and current Treasury chief of staff;

- Ed Liddy, former GS board member and Paulson-appointed AIG CEO;

- Gene Sperling, former Goldman consultant and Deputy Treasury Secretary under Robert Rubin;

- Robert Hormats, former vice chairman GS International; now Under Secretary of State for Economic, Business and Agricultural Affairs;

- Stephen Friedman, former Bush National Economic Council director, New York Fed board chairman, and Goldman chairman, now a Goldman board member;

- George Herbert Walker IV, former Goldman managing director, current mutual fund manager, and Bush family member;

- Mario Draghi, Governor of the Bank of Italy (2006–);

- Romano Prodi, Prime Minister of Italy (1996–1998, 2006–2008) and President of the European Commission (1999–2004);

- Mark Carney, Governor of the Bank of Canada;

- John Thain, former GS mortgage desk chief, CEO of the New York Stock Exchange, Merrill Lynch chairman and CEO, and now chairman and CEO of the CIT Group;

- numerous other prominent alums with ties to Washington, the New York Fed, and other institutions of power, including currently under Treasury Secretary Geithner.

Institutional Risk Analytics managing partner Christopher Whalen called Goldman's ties to the New York Fed "grotesque, [giving] the appearance of conflict of interest....everywhere." As Treasury Secretary, Paulson was unconstrained, stacking the agency with his cronies, then running it like a GS subsidiary.

A Brief Goldman Sachs History

- Founded by Marcus Goldman in 1869.

- In 1906, GS became a major player in the IPO (initial public offering) business.

- In 1929, Goldman is involved in the market crash, suffers big losses like others on the Street.

- In 1930, Sidney Weinberg (aka "Mr. Wall Street") becomes CEO.

- In 1956, GS is Ford's lead underwriter.

- In 1969, Gus Levy succeeds Weinberg.

- In 1976, John Weinberg (Sidney's son) succeeds Levy.

- In 1981, Goldman acquires J. Arons & Co., a commodities trading firm.

- In 1990, Robert Rubin and Stephen Friedman succeed J. Weinberg, expanding the company globally.

- In 1999, CEO and chairman Jon Corzine resigns as co-head, leaving Henry Paulson in charge.

- In 2006, Paulson becomes Treasury Secretary; Blankfein succeeds him.

- In 2008, Goldman becomes a bank holding company to get easier access to liquidity and funding.

- In 2009, Goldman had its most profitable ever year.

On Wall Street, past is always prologue. New scams follow old ones. Regulators look the other way. Washington acts as facilitator. Financialized America never had it better, especially firms like Goldman, manipulating markets easily for profits, besides scamming new generations of investors.

As sitting ducks, they're easily fleeced. It's a Wall Street tradition, with no firm more adept than Goldman, masters at profiting hugely from new scams. Investors beware.

Endnotes

1   Securities and Exchange Commission, "SEC Charges Goldman Sachs With Fraud in Structuring and Marketing of CDO Tied to Subprime Mortgages," April 16, 2010, available at <http://www.sec.gov/news/press/2010/2010-59.htm>

2   Steve Eder and Karey Wutkowski, "Goldman's 'Fabulous' Fab's confidential love letters," *Reuters*, April 25, 2010, available at <http://www.reuters.com/article/2010/04/25/us-goldman-emails-idUSTRE63O26E20100425>

11

FINANCIALIZATION

THE RISE OF
CASINO CAPITALISM

Giant corporations arose early in the last century followed by wars, depression, and more wars. Post-WW II, capitalism flourished, especially in America, unravaged by global conflict.

As a result, corporate America prospered, grew larger and more dominant. Profit-making oligopolies and monopolies resulted, competing more on innovative marketing than price. Surpluses and overcapacity resulted, making it essential to develop profit-making opportunities beyond traditional investment, production and consumption.

Beginning in the late 1960s, financialization came to the rescue, shifting economic control from industrial America to financial markets where the greatest high stakes games are played. Corporations were seen increasingly as bundles of assets, the more liquid the better. A new monopoly finance capitalism developed to exploit it.

It produced new FIRE sector (finance, insurance, and real estate) outlets for surpluses, mostly for speculation, not for capital goods investments in plant, equipment, transportation, and public utilities that had earlier fueled business cycle expansions. As a result, greater profit making opportunities were created, that had been less available before the late 1960s—but not without huge risks.

In the 1980s, debt expanded exponentially. In the 1970s, it was about one-and-a-half times GDP. By 1985, it was double, and by 2005, it was three-and-a-times GDP, rising, and approaching the $44 trillion global level. Thereafter, new financial instruments and markets proliferated. Casino capitalism thrived. Major players like Goldman Sachs took full advantage, profiting hugely from speculation, chicanery and fraud. Far more lay ahead the more markets were deregulated, a process Jimmy Carter began.

Much earlier, Keynes warned about "enterprise becom[ing] the bubble on a whirlpool of speculation" as it had in the 1920s, causing the Great Depression.

Beginning in the late 1960s, the economic malaise needed a new stimulus to reverse it. However, lacking profitable industrial opportunities, corporations sought them through financialization and speculation. The financial system responded with a bewildering array of new instruments, including stock futures, options, derivatives, hedge funds, and more.

Henceforth, instead of making better things for better living, America's New Economy proliferates an unbridled destructive greed, fueled by limitless amounts of privately created money, the root malignancy that is destroying the country.

As a result, a burgeoning financial superstructure has gained a life of its own. Today it's more dominant than ever, its epicenter on Wall Street, strip-mining global economies for profit, ripping off investors and homeowners for more, grabbing everything that smells of money.

Earlier, times were different. But when New Economy notions took hold, the sky was the limit. Bubbles grew that always burst. Minor by comparison, the 1997-98 Asian crisis showed how fast contagion could spread. Today it's global and more out-of-control than reported. Bad policy exacerbates it, sacrificing the economy longer term to bail out the banks. It's a hopelessly flawed strategy except for Wall Street where profits are burgeoning because rigged accounting rules conceal losses.

Moreover, Washington privatizes profits and socializes losses. It sacrifices Main Street for Wall Street, trying to pump life into a corpse through a sort of shell game or grandest of grand theft process of sucking wealth from the public to the top in hope that enough of it will work.

Speculation and debt need more of the same to prosper, but in the end it's a losing game. The greater the expansion, the harder the economy falls—especially when we're not making things and working Americans are exploited.

Since the 1970s, wages stagnated and lost purchasing power as inflation rose, eroding benefits like retirement savings. Household debt rose to compensate. Two wage-earners were needed to keep up. As a result, monopoly finance capital created an accumulation of misery, reverberating since the 2008 global collapse, exposing capitalism's dark side and destructive contradictions, particularly in its financialization form.

Today's finance capital is irrational, exploitive, and destructive, harming the global populations living under it. As a result, millions face devastation, human misery, and death. The threat is real, growing, and more dangerous than most people imagine, remember, or know how to contain, without totally reconstructing a broken system and replacing it with a workable one such as this book endorses, discussed in the last chapter.

Selling Out America to Wall Street

Money doesn't buy everything, but it buys influence, lots of it, from billions of dollars in political contributions. From 1998-2008 alone, Wall Street investment firms, commercial banks, hedge funds, real estate companies and insurance conglomerates (the FIRE sector) spent over $1.7 billion directly and another $3.4 billion on lobbyists, in return for which they:

- were freed from regulation;

- could speculate on financial derivatives and an alphabet soup of securitized garbage, including asset-backed securities (ABSs), mortgage-backed securities (MBSs), collateralized mortgage obligations (CMOs), collateralized debt obligations (CDOs), collateralized bond obligations (CBOs), credit default swaps (CDSs), and collateralized fund obligations (CFOs). Combined, they're sliced, diced, packaged, repackaged, and sold in tranches to sophisticated and ordinary investors, many unwittingly through mutual funds, 401(k)s, pensions, and the like;

- could merge commercial and investment banking and insurance operations;

- bilked investors and the public through fraudulent schemes; and

- got trillions of bailout dollars after engineering the economic crash.

For decades, Wall Street and successive governments colluded to defraud the public, using various schemes to transfer their wealth to the privileged. Carter spearheaded the deregulation Nixon and Ford began by hiring Alfred Kahn to head the Civil Aeronautics Board (CAB).

The 1978 Airline Deregulation Act followed. It dissolved the CAB, removed industry restraints, and eased consolidation. Subsequent bills deregulated trucking and railroads—the 1980 Motor Carrier Act and 1980 Staggers Rail Act, following the 1976 Railroad Revitalization and Regulatory Reform Act.

Carter also phased out interest rate deposit ceilings, and gave the Fed more power through the 1980 Depository Institutions and Monetary Control Act, removing New Deal restraints and enabling subsequent administrations to go further.

Under Reagan, energy deregulation followed, notably oil and gas, then electric utilities under GHW Bush and Clinton, the result being high prices, brownouts, and Enron-like scandals. Earlier, the 1982 Alternative Mortgage Transactions Parity Act led to exotic feature mortgages with adjustable rates or interest-only. They carry low "teaser" rates for several years, after which they're adjusted much higher, often making the loans unaffordable, especially for low-income, high-risk borrowers using subprime and Alt-A loans.

The 1982 Garn-St. Germain Depository Institutions Act deregulated thrifts and fueled fraud, so much so that the Savings and Loan crisis followed, hundreds of banks failed, and taxpayers got stuck with most of the $160 billion cost. In 1987, the Government Accountability Office (GOA) declared the S & L deposit insurance fund insolvent because of mounting bank failures.

In 1988, global regulators imposed minimum bank capital requirements, known as the Basel Accord or Basel I, which were enforced in the G-10 countries. (Now we're at Basel III.)

In 1989, the Financial Institutions Reform and Recovery Act abolished the Federal Home Loan Bank Board and FSLIC, transferring them to the Office of Thrift Supervision (OTS) and FDIC. It also created the Resolution Trust Corporation (RTC) to liquidate troubled assets, assume Federal Home Loan Bank Board insurance functions, and clean up a troubled system.

Clinton era telecommunications deregulation let media and telecommunication giants consolidate, gave new digital television broadcast spectrum space to current TV station owners, and let cable companies increase their local monopolies.

Unleashing the Banks

During the Great Depression, the Bank Act of 1933 (Glass-Steagall) had created the FDIC, insuring bank deposits up to $5,000 and separating commercial from investment banks and insurance companies, among other provisions to curb speculation.

Senator Carter Glass was its prime mover and got Senator Henry Steagall to go along by including his amendment to protect deposits. Glass believed banks should stick to lending, not speculate, deal, or hold corporate securities. He blamed them for the 1929 crash, subsequent bank failures, and the Great Depression. The Bank Act of 1933 passed quickly to curb that.

No longer since the neoliberal 1990s.

Later weakened, it still curbed abusive practices until it was repealed in 1999, permitting commercial and investment banks as well as insurance companies to combine. This facilitated the consolidated power, fraud and abuse that followed. Other deregulatory rules permitted off-balance sheet accounting to let banks hide liabilities.

Clinton's 1994 Reigle-Neal Interstate Banking and Branching Efficiency Act let bank holding companies operate in more than one state.

In 1996, the Fed reinterpreted Glass-Steagall to let bank holding companies earn up to 25% of their revenue from investment banking. The 1998 Citicorp-Travelers merger followed, combining a commercial/investment bank with an insurance company ahead of the 1999 Financial Services Modernization Act, also called the Gramm-Leach-Bliley Act (GLBA), authorizing it.

In 2000, the Commodity Futures Modernization Act (CFMA) passed, legitimizing swap agreements and other hybrid instruments, at the heart of today's problems by ending regulatory oversight of derivatives and leveraging that turned Wall Street more than ever into a casino.

It also contained the "Enron Loophole" for its "Enron On-Line," the first Internet-based commodities transaction system to let companies trade energy and other commodity futures unregulated, effectively licensing pillage and fraud. Enron took full advantage until its house of cards collapsed.

Further, it launched a menu of options, forwards, swaps, warrants, leaps, baskets, swaptions, and unregulated credit derivatives—notably, credit default swaps—facilitating out-of-control speculation.

As unregulated insurance bets between two parties on whether or not a company's bonds would default mounted, Ellen Brown asked in her April 11, 2008 article titled, "Credit Default Swaps: Evolving Financial Meltdown and Derivative Disaster Du Jour:" What if "the smartest guys in the room designed their credit default swaps [but] forgot to ask one thing—what if the parties on the other side of the bet don't have the money to pay up?"

In late 2007, when the financial crisis hit, they didn't, causing a "supersized bubble" to deflate.

Enacted New Deal reforms had prevented it. Deregulatory madness assured it and the subsequent continuing global economic fallout, including:

- unprecedented fraud

- insider trading

- misrepresentation

- Ponzi schemes

- false accounting

- obscenely high salaries and bonuses

- bilking investors, customers and homeowners, as well as embezzling and other forms of theft, including through loans designed to fail

- clear conflicts of interest

- lax enforcement of remaining regulatory measures

- market manipulation

- fraudulent financial products; and

- massive public deception

Worst of all, they got away with it, and still do,. Minimally they enjoyed $12.4 trillion in bailout money—free Fed-created money plus interest on Fed-held reserves.

The Absence of Regulatory Oversight

New Deal reforms were abandoned, important ones that had largely worked as intended. The Securities and Exchange Act of 1934 followed the Securities Act of 1933, requiring offers and security sales to be registered, pursuant to the Constitution's interstate commerce clause. Previously, they were governed by state laws, so-called "blue sky laws" to protect against fraud.

The 1934 law regulated secondary trading of financial securities and established the SEC under Section 4 to enforce the new Act, and later the 1939 Trust Indenture Act, the 1940 Investment Company Act, the Investment Advisors Act the same year, Sarbanes-Oxley of 2002, and the 2006 Credit Rating Agency Reform Act.

The SEC was established to enforce federal securities laws throughout the security industry, the nation's financial and options exchanges, and other electronic securities markets and instruments unknown in the 1930s, including derivatives and other forms of speculation. In principle, it's charged with uncovering wrongdoing, assuring investors aren't swindled, and keeping the nation's financial markets free from fraud and other abuses.

That was then, but no longer. Under Bush II and Obama, the SEC is more facilitator than enforcer, a paper tiger, not a guardian of the public trust. As a result, it:

- turned a blind eye to fraud and abuse

- protected Wall Street, not investors

- neutered its enforcement staff's authority

- adopted voluntary regulation

The SEC let investment banks:

- hold less reserve capital

- freely use leverage

- incur much higher debt levels, and

- operate freely, only occasionally punishing offenders with wrist-slaps too small to matter.

Financial fraud prosecutions dropped sharply, and were practically never launched against powerful, well-connected firms. Bernie Madoff was an exception because he told his sons after his house of cards collapsed. They turned him in for running what he called a "giant Ponzi scheme," similar to what Wall Street does but on a much smaller scale.

Obama exacerbated the worst bad practices. Wall Street gets a free ride. Foxes guard the hen house. Inmates run the asylum. Regulators don't regulate. Investigations aren't conducted. Criminal fraud is ignored. Nothing is done to curb it, and except for Madoff, only the small fries need worry. Washington protects the big ones, with Obama assigning Mary Schapiro the task as SEC chief.

A consummate insider, she spent years promoting Wall Street self-regulation, headed the Financial Industry Regulatory Authority (FINRA), was the National Association of Securities Dealers' (NASD) chairman, president, and CEO, ran the Commodity Futures Trading Commission, and is expert at quashing fraud investigations.

On her watch, honest due diligence is absent. A consummate insider, she was chosen to prevent it. Wall Street and the major media applauded her selection because of where her dominant interests lie.

Moreover, during America's golden age of pillage, regulators ignored predatory lending practices by:

- overriding state consumer protection laws to curb exploitive lending and other abuses;

- preventing victims from suing predatory loan issuers;

- freeing Fannie Mae, Freddie Mac, and giant Wall Street players to operate recklessly;

- letting them hide toxic assets by off-balance sheet accounting (Financial Accounting Standards Board rules allow it, and the Security Industry and Financial Markets Association and the American Securitization Forum lobbied furiously to keep them unchanged; in other words, to continue to deceive the public by letting insolvent institutions look healthy);

- letting them eliminate some of their own (Bear Stearns, Lehman Bros., Merrill Lynch and others) to remove competition;

- abandoning antitrust and other regulatory principles;

- creating too-big-to-fail institutions; and

- letting them operate freely, absent meaningful oversight.

Credit rating agencies played their part as well because of incestuous relationships with issuers. As a result, they ignored risky financial instruments, rated them highly, and duped investors to believe junk was safe. The SEC could have intervened but didn't. The 2006 Credit Rating Agencies Reform Act requires regulators to establish clear guidelines to determine which ones qualify as NRSROs (Nationally Recognized Statistical Rating Organizations).

The SEC is supposed to monitor their internal record-keeping and prevent conflicts of interest, but can't regulate their methodology and must approve their standards even knowing they're flawed.

One hand thus feeds the other. Regulators and credit agencies ignore abuses, cry foul when it's too late, then promise greater diligence next time. Change, of course, never comes, until everything unravels, it's too late, and financial wizards move on to other scams besides hanging on to old ones, some redesigned to look different.

After the 2008 Bear Stearns collapse, special lending facilities opened the discount window to investment banks, accepting a broad range of asset-backed securities, principally toxic ones, as collateral. Economist Michael Hudson calls them "cash for trash." Numerous other programs followed, including:

- the 2008 Emergency Economic Stabilization Act (ESSA) establishing the Troubled Asset Relief Program (TARP) to trade bad assets for good ones;

- the 2008 New York Fed administered Term Asset-Backed Securities Loan Facility (TALF) to lend up to $1 trillion on a non-recourse basis to holders of certain AAA-rated asset-backed securities (ABS) backed by newly and recently originated consumer and small business loans;

- Fed purchases of money market instruments;

- the Public-Private Investment Program (PPIP) to subsidize toxic asset purchases with government guarantees;

- multi-trillions of dollars in bank bailouts;

- near-zero interest rate loans; and

- QE I and II, ad infinitum until excesses get so extreme they collapse, crashing world economies with it.

Wall Street never had it so good. For Main Street, hard times are worsening as America sinks deeper into depression, a protracted one hitting the needy and disadvantaged hardest. The land of the free is more callous than ever, taking from the many for the few in an ongoing three-decades heist, sucking public wealth to the top since 2008 in unimaginable amounts.

As a result, you can expect

- a deepening global depression;

- protracted economic, political, social, and institutional upheaval;

- greater unemployment, poverty, homelessness, and hunger; and

- severe repression to curb public anger.

Blame it on decades of political influence-buying, yielding unprecedented returns for the privileged, but economic wreckage and catastrophic life changes for others, including the destruction of America's middle class. The price of excess is pain, lots of it for the world's disadvantaged, the ones who always pay dearly for rich peoples' crimes.

More Deregulatory Gutting for Business

On January 18, 2011, Obama's Executive Order (EO) "Improving Regulation and Regulatory Review" announced more deregulatory gutting to benefit business, no matter the public cost.

In a February 7 Chamber of Commerce speech, he elaborated, promising to "remove outdated, unnecessary regulations" to free business more than ever since the roaring twenties to do whatever they damn well please, saying:

> I understand the challenges you face. I understand you are under incredible pressure to cut costs and keep your margins up. I understand the significance of your obligations to your shareholders and the pressures that are created by quarterly reports. I get it.

What he doesn't "get" or give a damn about is growing human need. Instead, he focuses solely corporate bottom line concerns that no leader should prioritize over greater ones affecting millions of troubled households during the nation's gravest economic crisis in decades, one he's worsening, not alleviating.

In fact, acting more like one of them than one of us, he discussed various special favors he had in mind, including lowering corporate taxes and "breaking down some of the barriers that stand in the way of your success," eliminating "outdated and unnecessary regulations" to save billions of dollars annually, no matter the incalculable public cost. Dismissively, he said:

> I've ordered a government-wide review, and if there are rules on the books that are needlessly stifling job creation and economic growth, we will fix them...I've also ordered agencies to find ways to make regulations more flexible for small business,

promising to make government as accommodative as possible, giving away the store if there's anything left from the wreckage he already caused.

On May 26, 2011, Reuters writer Alister Bull headlined, "White House takes steps to cut business red tape," saying that Obama unveiled a plan to save corporations "billions of dollars over time, seeking to placate businesses complaining about what they see as undue regulatory burden."

Obama's "Simpler, Smarter Regulatory System"

Thirty federal agencies proposed eliminating or modifying hundreds of regulations to benefit business, despite compromising environmental concerns, sacrificing public safety, and disregarding general welfare issues.

While details so far are sketchy, several proposals include:

- excusing states from requiring air pollution vapor recovery systems at gas stations;

- ending "outdated" Endangered Species Act regulations;

- freeing business from 1.9 million regulatory reporting hours relating to workplace safety;

- curtailing railroad and other safety standards;

- stressing bottom line priorities over public benefits; and

- assuring further deregulation follows current proposals.

Office of Management and Budget (OMB) director Jacob Lew said:

Paperwork and reporting burdens are a serious problem...
This is not a one-time project. This is the beginning of
what will become a new way of doing business.

Responding, the Chamber of Commerce applauded "some commonsense recommendations that will save businesses some time, money, headaches, and resources," adding much more needs to be done:

What we need is a plan to make our flawed regulatory
system smarter, less intrusive, and more accountable.

National Resources Defense Council (NRDC) Legislative Director Scott Slesinger responded:

The purpose of the regulatory system is to protect
the health and well-being of the American public. Any
proposed changes should be closely evaluated to ensure
they protect the public, first and foremost.
Coming at a time when the entire system for
protecting [public safety] is already under political attack
by some in Congress, we will closely examine these specific
changes to ensure that federal agencies continue to put
the public's interest above all else.

From what's so far known, public safety and welfare are being sacrificed for bottom line considerations, with Obama prioritizing his efforts to address them.

Monetary Madness

Financial expert and investor safety advocate Martin Weiss devotes much of his time explaining how the global economic crisis brought the entire financial industry to its knees. In so doing, it caused the largest commercial, investment and consumer banking, brokerage, mortgage lending, and insurance companies to fail, or come close.

"Think about that," he said. "The world's largest companies in every sector of the financial industry. Failed. Bankrupt."

Now we're led to believe that "suddenly and miraculously" the crisis is over. The global economy regained health and resumed growing. Think again. The derivatives time bomb remains. So do the enormous bad debts on major banks' books. Most important, bad government and Fed policies continue unabated. As a result, Wall Street's debt crisis is now Washington's. This is what bankrupted giant financial firms are doing to America and other sovereign states.

Worst of all, said Weiss, the debt crisis is now a dollar one because Fed chairman Bernanke doubled the US monetary base in 112 days, and keeps expanding it. Not in 5,012 days as under his predecessors.

Most important, he caused "a massive, revolutionary change in the entire structure of the US economy"[1] by not using it for productive growth—a shocking indictment of Bernanke's gross malfeasance, saving Wall Street at the expense of the economy.

As the new millennium approached, the Fed increased the monetary base by $73 billion in three months to deal with a potential Y2K bug. After 9/11, another $40 billion was added in less than two weeks. Compare that with Bernanke, who created over $1 trillion in less than four months, plus additional hundreds of billions afterward—none or very little, however, for productive growth.

Moreover, after the Y2K and 9/11 crises passed, the Fed promptly reversed its monetary infusions by withdrawing the extra liquidity added. Bernanke did the opposite. As a result, the monetary base reached all-time highs and keeps expanding.

From September 2008 to February 2009, it exploded by $1.3 trillion under QE I, his quantitative easing policy. QE II followed, adding an announced $600. In fact, it exceeded $900 billion, beginning months earlier than announced.

At the same time, Bernanke promised an "exit strategy," when, in fact, none exists, just more binge money creation because "inflation is too low" when, in fact, it's much higher than rigged CPI numbers. Anyone buying food, fuel, electricity, health insurance, prescription drugs, and other daily essentials, besides paying rent and college tuitions, understands what government data conceal. America's cost of living is high, rising, and for growing millions, unaffordable.

In February 2011, Institutional Risk Analytics' Christopher Whalen said: The longer the Fed bails out banks and artificially keeps credit cheap, "the worse our collective predicament."[2]

Analyst Martin Mayer once admonished the Fed not to do harm. Instead, Bernanke fueled food, energy, strategic commodities, and equity market bubbles on an ocean of out-of-control liquidity. Moreover, as Mayer explained, he jeopardized economic stability by making "an end run around the authority of the legislature." No wonder a worried Dallas Fed President, Richard Fisher, said in November 2010:

I take no comfort, and see considerable risk, in conducting

monetary policy that has the consequence of transferring income from the poor and the worker and the saver to the rich. Senior citizens and others who saved by the rules are earning nothing on their savings, while big debtors and too-big-to-fail oligopoly banks benefit from their subsidy.[3]

Believing Bernanke lost all credibility, other policy makers and analysts feel the same way, but unfortunately they're far outnumbered. Make no mistake, however. Sooner or later, this chicken's coming home to roost. Rising gold and silver prices, falling dollar valuations, insolvent states and cities, growing poverty, high unemployment, and other distress signs reflect it. Today's recovery is illusory. Chapter 8 highlighted it, saying the recession is over, the depression just beginning. Main Street's felt it all along.

As a result, Bernanke and Greenspan will be remembered as America's two worst Fed chairmen, responsible for wrecking America, by not furthering prosperous long-term growth. They believe that is unimportant as long as Wall Street thrives.

Endnotes

1   Martin D. Weiss, "Massive Revolutionary Changes," *Money and Markets*, November 9, 2009, available at <http://www.moneyandmarkets.com/massive-revolutionary-changes-36311>

2   Christopher Whalen, "Why the Fed must let rates rise," *Reuters*, April 26, 2011, available at <http://blogs.reuters.com/christopher-whalen/>

3   Richard Fisher, "Recent Decisions of the Federal Open Market Committee: A Bridge to Fiscal Sanity?" Remarks before the Association for Financial Professionals, San Antonio, Texas, November 8, 2010, available at <http://www.dallasfed.org/news/speeches/fisher/2010/fs101108.cfm>

12

CLASS WARFARE JEOPARDIZING AMERICAN WORKERS' SECURITY

Warren Buffett once said: "There's class warfare, all right, but it's my class, the rich class, that's making war, and we're winning," Obama's deficit-cutting agenda is the latest battle.

On May 4, 2010, Hugo Radice, Life Fellow of the University of Leeds School of Politics and International Studies, headlined an article, "Cutting Public Debt: Economic Science or Class War?" asking:

> Is cutting the public debt really an objective economic necessity, or is it actually a deeply political stance, reflecting the interests of the business and financial elites?

Analyzing historical public policies, he explained the shift from earlier Keynesianism to "the unchallenged hegemony of free-market neoliberalism since the early 1990s." In fact, over the past three decades, the shift was notable, beginning under Britain's Margaret Thatcher and America's Ronald Reagan, establishing practices that succeeding administrations deepened. As a result, Britain's New Labour governs like Conservatives while American Democrats mimic Republicans, especially on imperial and pocket book issues.

Radice calls it class warfare, pitting private wealth against public good, instilling "a new common sense" based on property rights, individualism, and the notion that free markets work best so let them, including the right to demand massive public spending cuts, ones Radice says "are not, repeat not, economically necessary."

Nonetheless, for over 30 years, such cuts have been ongoing. Since the mid-1970s, real wages haven't kept pace with inflation. Benefits have steadily eroded. High-paying jobs disappeared. Improved technology forced wage earners to work harder for less. More than ever, "free" markets work only for those who control them.

As a result, the class struggle between haves and have-nots escalated. A handful of powerful winners emerged. Wealth disparity extremes became unprecedented. Exploitation increased and successive crises, with busts following speculative booms. Easy credit fueled all this by excessive lending and spending as well as high public and private debt levels. To heal, officials now call for "shared sacrifice," their sharing, our sacrifice.

Richard Wolff calls mainstream economics "faith-based." For Michael Hudson it's "junk economics," a Wall Street power grab, holding industrial America and wage earners hostage, with debt peonage as the final solution, benefitting only a powerful, elite few.

Today's buzzword across Europe and America is austerity. Obama's deficit commission has declared war on ordinary workers, targeting their jobs, benefits, standard of living, and retirement futures with draconian cuts. It's a scam to transfer greater wealth to the rich, looting multi-trillions—the grandest of grand theft, class warfare of the worst kind, a bipartisan scheme to wreck the economy and working Americans' lives for profit.

After endorsing Obama's deficit commission proposals, a November 11, 2010 *New York Times* editorial headlined "Waiting for the President" said there's "no way to wrestle the deficit under control without both cutting spending and raising taxes." Everything "must be on the table," with Obama out in front promoting it. Watching from the sidelines increases the odds "it will never go anywhere." Strong White House leadership is needed to support "the commission's plain truths."

The editorial, along with other mainstream opinions and Obama's deficit cutters, avoided constructive alternatives on the right way to address high debt, foster economic growth, and lift all boats equitably. Some obvious ones that another chapter discusses include:

- waging war on concentrated wealth and power;

- adopting an across-the-board populist agenda, elevating social justice as issue one;

- slashing the defense budget, minimally in half, ideally much more, including closing overseas bases, reducing force levels, ending foreign occupations, and renouncing imperial wars;

- implementing a progressive income tax, replacing today's dysfunctional one;

- removing the payroll tax ceiling, taxing all earned income at the same rate;

- empowering workers to bargain collectively with management on equal terms;

- legislating a guaranteed living wage, adjusted by urban, rural, state and local considerations;

- implementing a guaranteed income for the indigent;

- undertaking real regulatory reform, reinstituting vital ones eroded or lost;

- abolishing monopoly and oligopoly power;

- strengthening public education;

- enacting universal, single-payer healthcare, excluding predatory insurers, except as a voluntary option;

- returning money creation power to Congress as the Constitution mandates;

- instituting a Tobin Tax to make Wall Street and rich investors pay their fair share.

This would do much toward establishing democratic government of, by, and for the people

Benefits of a Tobin Tax

Besides discouraging speculation, economist Robert Pollin estimates that a tax of one-half of one percent can raise about $350 billion annually. A one-tenth of one percent tax on the estimated $500 trillion in annual derivatives trades could bring up to $500 billion a year.

Depending on volumes and taxable trading threshold levels, those figures might be greater or smaller but they are nonetheless considerable. If used wisely by government, they'd help grow the economy productively, cut the deficit, and raise everyone's standard of living equitably, especially that of working Americans who are presently left out of bipartisan consideration—corrupted for America's aristocracy, mostly, of course, for corrupted Wall Street giants.

Instead ordinary Americans are sacrificed on the altar of capitalist excess, their pain the price for its gain, a shocking indictment of a broken system. In fact, it's venal, depraved, degenerate, and criminal, deserving a dagger in its heart to kill it before making workers serfs, and destroying their retirement security.

America's Growing Retirement Crisis

In the May 2006 issue of *Monthly Review*, Teresa Ghilarducci titled her article "The End of Retirement," saying: "Scarcely a day passes without a new pension nightmare: Social Security privatization," corporations ending private pensions, declining household savings, cancelled retirement healthcare benefits, and "401(k) accounts becoming '201(k)s,'" having replaced traditional pensions. Defined benefit obligations are fast disappearing.

These developments reflect a nightmarish reality. Today's "ownership society" forces everyone to manage their financial futures, leaving them vulnerable to marketplace uncertainties. It's a task few can handle, especially during hard times, which are eroding years of saved resources savagely, that older workers maybe can't recoup.

Conditions are far worse today than in May 2006. Yet, Ghilarducci said, "For the first time in US history, every source of retirement income is under siege: Social Security, personal savings, and occupational pensions." Also Medicare for retirees, their dependents, and the disabled, as well as Medicaid for the nation's poor—vital income-equivalent plans without which millions would be uninsured or underinsured, leaving them vulnerable to catastrophic illness costs.

In July 2010, Professor James W. Russell, writing in *Socialism and Democracy*, titled his article, "Retirement Crisis in the United States," saying: "The great 30-year experiment in 401(k) and similar retirement financing schemes that depend on stock market investments has failed." Even before the 2008 crash, it was clear, the signs were "everywhere that very few workers would be able to accumulate enough wealth through these accounts to insure" their retirement futures.

Like Russell, economist Richard Wolff explains that until 1980, each generation since the 19th century was better off financially than previous ones, including having more retirement security. No longer. Workers have since been victimized by institutionalized inequality. They've faced eroded union representation, mostly in commerce and industry, stagnant wages, weakened or lost benefits, and high-risk defined contribution pension plans replacing secure defined benefit ones.

By 1935, during the Great Depression, 34 European nations and America had established social insurance programs. It was a watershed time, "consistent with the socialist value of solidarity through socialization of support for children, the elderly, the disabled, and others unable to" work productively for a living.

Social Security in America as Amended

The Social Security Act became law when Franklin Roosevelt signed it on August 14, 1935, perhaps his finest hour, implementing a measure during hard times against the 50% poverty rate. They're still hard with US poverty rates soaring, perhaps heading for Great Depression levels or higher.

Social Security works well as mandated, taxing active workers and their employers to support eligible retirees, their dependents and the disabled. As Russell explains: "It is a formula that has worked remarkably well since its inception, producing the federal government's most successful and popular domestic program."

Employers also began offering pensions in a package of other benefits. It worked the same way; they and workers contributed for retirees, using a "pay-as-you-go formula"—simple, effective, and assured, based on employment tenure under individual company plans.

The Revenue Act of 1978, however, changed things. Its sections 401(k), 403(b), and 457 let retirement plan contributions be made with pretax dollars. Though intended to encourage worker participation in defined benefit plans, employers used it advantageously, increasingly switching them to defined contribution ones, providing no assurance of enough retirement income.

In contrast, "defined benefit plans are progressive reforms within capitalist societies that are consistent with guaranteeing old age support as worker or social rights." Today, they're fast disappearing, victimized by neoliberal "reforms" for business, especially financial industry predators, not employees.

Russell cites two reasons why 401(k)s failed:

- They falsely assume worker investments (mostly stock market ones) are risk free and will provide a secure retirement.

- They presume that, given other lifetime obligations, including medical expenses, home purchases, mortgage payments, and college tuitions, these investments are possible for most people and will be wisely made.

The financial services industry profits hugely from private investment plans, siphoning off large commission amounts that add up through the years; as a result, American workers have subsidized the industry's expansion while jeopardizing their own futures.

In actuality, government- or business-provided plans that purport to be "dedicated purely to supporting retirement instead of creating private wealth," often function more for the benefit of investment firms than their customers, and therein lies the problem. Instead of providing secure retirement income, they depend on the marketplace which is full of uncertainty that in crisis times can be ruthless, destroying years of savings quickly, savagely, and unfairly.

As a result, for millions, 401(k)s and similar plans have been poison, failing to deliver on promises. Three arguments were made to sell them:

- They would far outperform traditional pensions—untrue.

- Retirement income would be "owned"—true, but it hardly matters if it is insufficient or at risk.

- They'd be portable—importantly true in a highly mobile society where jobs and careers change more often than earlier.

A major problem is how commonly these plans are used for home purchases, medical expenses, college tuitions, other needs, or discretionary ones, depleting funds intended for retirement.

In contrast, Social Security works as intended by financing it, not by private wealth or to make profits for financial services or stock market predators. Bogusly, critics claim it's going bankrupt when, in fact, it's sound and secure if properly administered, needing only modest adjustments at times to keep it that way.

Moreover, as explained above, simple revenue enhancement methods exist, including a progressive income tax; removing the payroll tax ceiling, taxing all earned income at the same rate; and instituting a Tobin Tax. Combined, they might keep Social Security flourishing for a millennium, for sure a century, two, or longer.

As Russell pointed out, "There could and should be [ways to expand] Social Security benefits and [begin] phas[ing] out employment-based retirement plans" that don't deliver on promises. Retirement plans should have fundamental goals—to provide secure, predictable, adequate income amounts, adjusted for inflation, delivering as much annual working lifetime earnings as possible.

Achieving it depends on replacing today's "three-legged stool"— "Social Security, employment-based benefit(s), and personal savings— with a national system in which Social Security accounts for" the lion's share of income, "topped off by personal savings" that for most people are meager.

A Final Comment

For American workers, achieving retirement security is simple and achievable, but not with opposition from powerful, destructive forces—

financial giants complicit with government, willing bipartisan congressional majorities plotting to jeopardize the future of millions. Chapter 7 explained how.

Only mass outrage can stop them from slashing Social Security, Medicare, Medicaid, and other social benefits on the way to ending them—a venal plot to make America a banana republic, its working millions oppressed serfs, with their present and future security destroyed.

Obama and congressional majorities support this in league with their big money backers, largely Wall Street racketeers, who are profiting hugely from sucking public and personal wealth to themselves. The die is cast. It's their future or ours. There's no in between. Grassroots activism only—or lack of it—will decide.

13

WAGING WAR ON AMERICAN WORKERS

Target Number One is America's middle class, endangered after decades of wealth shifts to super-rich elites, with besides most high-paying, good benefit jobs being offshored to cheap labor markets—a policy Washington's congressional duopoly endorses. It's the most serious threat to middle America since the attacks began in the 1970s.

On December 23, 1957, The Dan Smoot Report published an article titled "Honoria," by novelist Taylor Caldwell (1900-1985), about the true story of a formerly great nation and the lessons to be learned from its demise.

Caldwell explained how in Honoria, men seeking freedom became Pilgrims, endured terrible hardships, yet survived, prospered, and gained power. They established colonies, believed in God, hard work, public education, and transformed villages into towns and cities.

Others joined them, establishing new colonies, then uniting them. A civil war intervened. The republic was divided. A leader was assassinated, but prosperity followed conflict resolution. However, arrogance, corruption, and foreign entanglements followed. At issue—insatiable greed, not defending civilized world freedoms.

Wars resulted. Repressive laws were passed, but the nation of Honoria had "a strong, industrious middle class, composed of farmers, artisans, [and] shopkeepers." However, they posed a threat to wealth and power so they had to go to let the elites rule unchallenged. Targeted by oppression, they "were reduced to despair," and began "dwindl[ing] away... Morality was dead."

The monstrous bureaucratic state "was happy." People wanted entertainment, not freedom. Leaders waged more wars. Honoria became more corrupt and extremist. Its middle class eroded, died, and barbarians moved in.

Who was to blame? "Honoria, of course," at the expense of its own citizens. Once they had sacrificed for the common good but as they let down their guard, they were betrayed. Over hundreds of years, Honoria rose and fell. Its real name? "Ancient Rome." America is its modern equivalent.

America, the New Rome

As constitutional freedoms and middle class prosperity erode, America is slowly dying. The two empires, America and Rome, share a remarkably common history. Both rose and prospered, then became overextended, rushed toward the abyss, and couldn't turn back. America is on its edge. Its belligerence exceeds Rome's. Its excesses are unsustainable. Its middle class is dying, its democracy a mere figure of speech.

Today, super-wealth rules a once great nation that is malignant with corruption, delusional with notions of grandeur, and of might ideologically triumphing over right. It's a self-destructive path harming working Americans most, especially the once vibrant middle class, which is targeted for destruction. Democracy depends on preserving it as a buffer against tyranny. Slowly, however, the American middle class is suffocating and dying, and with it, the remnants of freedom.

A New Congress Highlights an Accelerated Ruinous Path

On January 3, the 112th Congress convened with an agenda that will accelerate America's ruin.

In 2011, federal and state governments plan major social services cuts and other ways to address deficit and budget problems through less social spending, layoffs, and other draconian measures. At the same time, America's aristocracy is flourishing, largely at the expense of exploited workers. Their assets flow upward to make super-rich society richer, facilitated by bipartisan political complicity and corruption.

House Republicans want budget cuts of $100 billion, largely on the backs of working Americans who can least afford it. Given Obama's austerity pledge, bipartisan agreement may target entitlements, including Social Security, Medicare and Medicaid, as well as education, transportation, and other discretionary areas to match 2008 levels. However, achieving it requires 20% cuts across the board from the $477 billion Congress allocated in FY 2010, ending September 30.

According to House Budget Committee chairman Paul Ryan, "That's where you get the savings." On January 6, he also told Bloomberg News that potential state defaults won't be saved by bailouts. "We are not interested in a bailout," he said.

In 1933, at the height of the Great Depression, Arkansas was the last state to default at a time when Washington rescues weren't considered. Today, workers will be punished to assure steady debt service payments. In 2009, California state treasurer Bill Lockyer said only a "thermonuclear war" might force default, nothing less.

Less draconian than Republicans, congressional Democrats, at least rhetorically, want FY 2010 spending levels frozen for three years. House Republicans, however, control appropriations so expect debt ceiling level confrontations. For one thing, Republicans want spending increases to be offset by cuts, meaning those affecting working Americans most.

They'll come at a time that analysis by the Economic Policy Institute (EPI), evaluating poverty in the "Great Recession," shows over 21% of Americans are in poverty. Calling official measures outdated, it derives its conclusions from after-tax market wages and salaries, excluding entitlements, welfare, and other government programs that lower the figure considerably but not for millions not helped. Then, to this measurement of poverty based on income, add on the deficit side, the higher cost of living expenses, especially for health care, food, gasoline, heating oil, and rent at a time when home prices are declining.

With planned FY 2011 budget cuts, greater poverty looms ahead. On January 6, even the Census Bureau raised its numbers, saying 15.7% of the population (not 14.3%) lived in poverty in 2009, or 47.8 million people. Moreover, despite Social Security and Medicare, 16.1% of seniors are impoverished when out-of-pocket medical and other expenses are included. Children are most impacted at 18%, nearly one-fifth of them. A 2009 EPI report estimated one in four, and for Blacks and Hispanics, well over one in three.

In fact, Census Bureau figures far understate reality. Its poverty threshold, for example, is based on an annual $22,050 income for a family of four. Yet urban needs throughout America are much higher. According to a 2007 EPI report, a Chicago family of four needs over $49,000, and in New York, over $72,000.

Yet even official data offer insight into America's worst economic crisis since the Great Depression at a time when a bipartisan consensus plans social spending cuts when large increases are needed. Even so, public outrage is strangely absent. For how long is at issue.

States Plan Major Budget Cuts and Layoffs

Though the figures are slightly lower than in 2009 and 2010, the National Conference of State Legislatures forecasts $83 billion in combined state deficits (less than half other $175 billion estimates and rising), requiring greater cuts than earlier, absent federal government help or too little. As a result, major public spending cuts, wage freezes, and lower benefits are planned. Moreover, public employee unions are targeted, threatening organized labor overall.

On January 3, 2011, *New York Times* writer Steven Greenhouse headlined, "Strained States Turning to Laws to Curb Labor Unions," saying:

> Faced with growing budget deficits and restive taxpayers, elected officials from Maine to Alabama, Ohio to Arizona, are pushing new legislation to limit the power of labor unions, particularly those representing government workers, in collective bargaining and politics.

Though largely weak and ineffective, private sector unions are also being attacked. For example, lawmakers in Indiana, Maine, Missouri and at least seven other states plan legislation to bar them from requiring rank and file members to pay dues or fees, reducing union treasury funds.

Ohio's Republican Governor John Kasich and party bosses staged an unprecedented coup by replacing two GOP committee dissenters with supportive ones to get a full floor vote to strip public workers of collective bargaining rights and force them to take other benefit reductions.

In Wisconsin, Republican Governor Scott Walker and party bosses did the same thing by other means, ramming through a union busting bill despite Democrat and statewide opposition.

In both states, corrupted union bosses weakly contested it. For decades, they've been on the take, siding with business, getting big salaries and fancy perks, being more concerned about self-enrichment than rank and file member rights. Labor historian Paul Buhle sees organized labor in a state of collapse. In the March/April 2010 *Against the Current* issue, his article titled, "Labor at War or in the Tank," explained "the shrinking world of US organized labor," saying, "...a paucity of anything like solidarity, let alone a strategy for a repowered, reorganized, 21st-century labor movement" haunts American worker struggles going forward.

Moreover, recent reports suggest possible bankruptcy for "any number of the international unions as well as the AFL-CIO at large, a situation made only worse by infighting. This is a bleak irony, indeed, following so much enthusiasm" over Obama's election.

All the more reason for new leadership, information and insight to "be brought to rank-and-file working people within the unions and outside." In addition, add strong political support. At this time it's totally absent, with Democrats as anti-labor as Republicans.

On January 6, 2011 on the Progressive Radio News Hour, James

Petras explained that in 2008, Big Labor contributed over $400 million to Democrat candidates and tens of millions more in 2010. In return, Obama and congressional Democrats waged war on working Americans, endorsing layoffs, wage and benefit cuts, gutted work rules, and lost pensions. They promised hope from the Employee Free Choice Act (EFCA). The Democrat-controlled Congress then rejected it.

It would have been the first pro-labor reform since the landmark 1935 Wagner Act, letting workers for the first time bargain collectively with management on even terms. Though modest by comparison, it promised progress at a time organized labor is virtually impotent, because union bosses, like Democrats, side more with business than with their own rank and file.

Trapped in a malaise compounded by huge budget cuts, layoffs, and other social sacrifices, American workers face greater poverty, extended hard times, disenfranchisement, and bleaker futures. Moreover, their pensions are under attack. In December 2010, the Brookings Institution's Douglas J. Elliott headlined, "State and Local Pension Funding Deficits: A Primer," saying that by some measures national shortfalls exceed "$3 trillion or more than two years' worth of state and local tax revenues." Today's economic crisis revealed "the severity of the investment risks by very substantially increasing the gap between the value of [pension] assets accumulated [and] the value of pension promises" already made. Major underfunding and eroded investments are core issues of the problem. No easy solutions can resolve them.

Even at overvalued levels, "the stock market would have to almost triple" to close deficits "as measured using risk-free discount rates." Reforms are also needed, including in "accounting and actuarial rules so that state and local pension plans report liability levels and deficits that are consistent with economic reality," such as discounting "the uncertainty of the liabilities rather than the expected return on the assets" that don't materialize in hard times.

Worker Rights Threatened

Across America at the federal, state, and local levels, governments are taking action against worker's rights. Since taking office in January 2009, the Obama administration spurned them, while giving at least $12.4 trillion to Wall Street crooks and hundreds of billions more to other corporate favorites. At the same time, he stiff-armed budget-strapped states and local governments, especially in the current fiscal year, leaving them on their own to sink or swim.

He also did little for distressed households. Promising millions of new jobs, he created few, leaving real unemployment over 22% greater than three years after economic crisis began.

Moreover, he provided little popular aid overall, and facilitated Wall Street's home foreclosure racket, involving fabricated documents, forgery, perjury, lost paperwork, and "rocket docket" eviction speed-throughs lasting 20 seconds on average to approve. He also froze federal worker wages and plans sweeping austerity for working households, while showering business and America's aristocracy with generous tax breaks and other handouts.

Just as reactionary governors and mayors hammer their residents, Obama is hammering America. He's no friend of labor. In mid-February, he cynically told Milwaukee's WTMJ television that "Everybody's got to make some adjustments to new fiscal realities," claiming worker sacrifices are necessary to "save jobs" when, in fact, they're killing jobs and driving millions into poverty from wage and benefit cuts. At the same time, corporate profits are better than ever, achieved on the backs of hammered workers, swindled by a Washington/business cabal, sacrificing people for marketplace sovereignty—a government-sponsored racket.

Overall, Obama pretends to support workers. In fact, he spurns them, his vague, tepid rhetoric a dead giveaway for supporting class warfare, especially when backed up by harsh measures to quell dissent.

Extremist Think Tanks and Media Assault Worker Rights

Numerous right-wing think tanks infest America's landscape, generously funded by conservative foundations, including the Koch Family Foundations (established by David, Charles and Claude R. Lambe), several Scaife ones, the John M. Olin Foundation, Lynde and Harry Bradley Foundation, Smith Richardson Foundation, various others, and George Soros' Open Society Foundations, pretending to be liberal, when, in fact, he supports everything smelling of money.

Their agenda includes:

- marketplace sovereignty,

- deregulation,

- privatization of government services,

- ending popular entitlements, social spending, and affirmative action,

- prioritizing business friendly policies,

- waging class war,

- controlling electoral politics, and

• supportive media backing everything on their wish list.

Among many others, their beneficiaries include the American Enterprise Institute, Cato Institute, Club for Growth, Federalist Society, Heritage Foundation, Manhattan Institute for Policy Research, and Hoover Institution on War, Revolution and Peace, founded in 1919 by Herbert Hoover, best known for inaction while America sank into depression while he was president.

The Hoover Institution's notorious members include Condoleezza Rice, George Shultz, Edwin Meese, Margaret Thatcher, William Perry, Thomas Sowell, Shelby Steele, Michael Boskin, James Woolsey, Christopher Hitchens, Milton Friedman until he died, and Robert Barro, whose *Wall Street Journal* op-ed attacking collective bargaining is discussed below, and is typical of what Hoover members advocate.

Its mission statement endorses representative government and private enterprise, its definition of peace and personal freedom is tied to safeguarding America's system, benefitting wealth and power, not popular, interests.

Herbert Hoover's 1959 statement guides policy, saying that America's

> social and economic systems are based on private enterprise from which springs initiative and ingenuity... Ours is a system where the Federal Government should undertake no governmental, social or economic action, except where local government, or the people, cannot undertake it for themselves. [Safeguarding] the American system, [based on] individual, economic, and political freedom; private enterprise; and representative government...

This is fundamental to bedrock Hoover principles, ones very much anti-labor.

Less known anti-labor groups include:

American Crossroads

Founded by Karl Rove, it's "dedicated to renewing America's commitment to individual liberty, limited government, free enterprise, and a strong national defense," entirely benefitting business at the expense of workers.

Americans for Job Security

An anti-labor insurance industry front group backing unrestricted free enterprise, tax cuts for the rich, job-killing trade agreements, and the ending of worker rights for greater profits.

The Club for Growth

A neofascist organization wanting Medicare and Medicaid abolished, Social Security privatized, unions eliminated, and business given unimpeded power to plunder and exploit freely.

Americans for Prosperity

A virulently anti-labor group backing all of the above and more, including the right to destroy US jobs by offshoring them freely to the world's lowest wage locations.

Freedom Works

Led by former Republican House Majority Leader Dick Armey, it conducts aggressive campaigns against worker rights nationally.

Center for Union Facts

Led by pro-business lobbyist Richard Berman, it focuses on anti-union propaganda, destroying worker rights, obstructing organizing efforts, and promoting other anti-union initiatives.

National Right to Work Foundation and Committee

America's oldest anti-union organization, it bogusly claims pro-worker credentials. In fact, it's extremely hostile to high wages, essential benefits, job safety, and favorable working conditions, considered impediments to profits.

Public Service Research Foundation and Public Service Research Council

Composed of small organizations nationwide, they oppose collective bargaining rights for teachers and other public sector workers. In 1981, PSRF led the campaign to fire PATCO strikers, a watershed event weakening organized labor overall.

For-Profit Unionbusters

Describing themselves as "union avoidance firms," "management consultants," or "labor consultants," they use lawyers and other credentialed professionals to manipulate labor laws to subvert organizing efforts and worker rights overall.

These and other groups have full-time staffs, lawyers, and other credentialed professionals conducting media campaigns, seminars, workshops, lobbying efforts, and other initiatives to subvert organized labor for business. Nothing unethical is avoided to accomplish ends they'll go to any extreme to achieve, within or outside the law they freely exploit advantageously. And they are flush with cash to do it.

Annually, they spend tens of millions of dollars for anti-union initiatives, allied with the US Chamber of Commerce— "the world's largest business federation representing the interests of more than 3 million businesses of all sizes, sectors, and regions, as well as state and local chambers and industry associations."

Although most of its members are small enterprises, the US Chamber of Commerce overwhelmingly represents giant ones and their campaign for unimpeded free enterprise at the expense of worker rights and small competitors. As a result, it spends millions of dollars annually opposing the latter.

So did Milton Friedman. He said markets work best unfettered by rules, regulations, onerous taxes, trade barriers, "entrenched interests" and human interference, and the best government is practically none at all as anything it can do, private business does better. Democracy and government of, by and for the people? Heresy for Friedman, an ideology he taught and endorsed. Chapter 2 discussed it in detail.

Extremist economists like him endorse the same policies, wanting America returned to 19th century harshness. Acolyte Robert Barro is one.

On February 28, 2011, his *Wall Street Journal* op-ed headlined, "Unions vs. the Right to Work," saying, "Labor unions like to portray collective bargaining as a basic civil liberty, akin to the freedoms of speech, press, assembly and religion," mocking the most fundamental labor right without which no others exist.

The landmark 1935 Wagner Act lets unions bargain collectively with management on even terms, but that was a goal that was never achieved and has now been gravely weakened after decades of major erosion.

Ideally, collective bargaining seeks to level the playing field to resolve worker-management conflicts, and as such, represents an equitable industrial jurisprudence system, by including civil rights issues and establishing them in workplaces.

It thus counters one-sided management authority, limits its arbitrary decision making, strengthens worker rights, increases their self-respect, morale and productivity, enhances unionism, promotes fairness, and facilitates equitable labor-management resolutions, benefiting both sides by establishing open communications to achieve workplace harmony and peace.

Not according to Barro, who calls it "more similar to an antitrust violation than to a civil liberty," an astonishing mischaracterization by a Harvard economist playing politics, with sound economics left out of his assessment.

Pre-1935 when labor had no rights, workers were subject to the 1890 Sherman Antitrust Act guidelines, which were then removed by the 1914 Clayton Antitrust Act and Wagner Act (the 1935 National Labor Relations Act).

Barro endorses the 1947 Taft Hartley Act legislation, letting states pass right-to-work laws. Twenty-two mostly Southern and Western states now have them, prohibiting union-management agreements making membership or union dues an employment condition, before or after hiring.

Barro's convoluted reasoning claims the right to work trumps worker rights, and besides, it "has a much more pleasant, liberal sound than 'collective bargaining.' "

So does neoliberal, an extremist ideology Barro endorses, advocating marketplace sovereignty, profits over people, maintenenance of a large reserve army of labor to restrain wages and benefits, privatizing state resources, deregulation, slashing social services, and militant enforcement when necessary.

Anti-labor laws in Wisconsin, Ohio and other states, says Barro, "stem from the collision between overly generous benefits for public employees—notably for pensions and health care—and the fiscal crises of state and local governments," omitting that years of Wall Street shenanigans created them.

"Teachers and other public-employee unions went too far," said Barro, another astonishing misstatement that is contrary to the facts. Public workers, in fact, are under-, not over-compensated compared to their private sector counterparts.

Using Census Bureau data, a National Institute on Retirement Security (NIRS) study titled, "Out of Balance? Comparing Public and Private Sector Compensation Over 20 Years" concludes:

> Wages and salaries of state and local employees are lower
> than those for private sector employees with comparable
> earnings determinants, such as education and work
> experience. State workers typically earn 11 percent less
> and local workers 12 percent less.[1]

"During the last 15 years, the pay gap" widened. The pattern holds for most large states. "Benefits make up a slightly larger share of compensation for the state and local sector." Nonetheless, based on total compensation, state workers earn 6.8% less, and for local ones it's 7.4%.

University of Wisconsin-Madison Economics Professors Keith Bender and John Heywood co-authored the study, saying:

These public sector employees earn less than they would earn if they took their skills to the private sector.

Maybe Harvard economist Barro should take one of their classes to learn some real economic facts he either doesn't know or won't teach, his students losing out from a man endorsing union-busting extremism, who called Wisconsin's bill "fiscal reality." In fact, it's fiscal fascism, substituting right-to-work zealotry for collective bargaining fairness.

No matter. Barro urged politicians to match Walker by "maintain[ing] their resolve [to] achieve a more sensible long-term structure for the taxpayers in their states."

Many of these taxpayers, in fact, are public employees, the same ones making state and local governments work. Like all working Americans, they deserve fair pay and benefits for it, not Barro's "fiscal reality," heading them for neoserfdom everywhere this fascist legislation passes.

A Final Comment

Working Americans, especially middle class ones, are being downsized toward extinction through loss of high pay/good benefit jobs, labor rights, political empowerment, standard of living gains, personal freedoms, and retirement futures.

Replacing private pensions with 401(k)s, IRAs and similar schemes failed.Public pensions now face a similar fate, with states wanting liability shifted from them to workers, leaving workers vulnerable and on their own. It's consistent with destructive neoliberal "reforms," wanting all public benefits eroded and eliminated. The scheme is venal and underhanded— intended to create a ruler-serf society, reducing America to a third world status of super-wealth and growing poverty extremes. Bipartisan political support, in fact, endorses the process.

Endnotes

1   Keith Bender and John Heywood, *Out of Balance? Comparing Public and Private Sector Compensation Over 20 Years*," National Institute on Retirement Security, April 2010, available at <http://www.nirsonline.org/storage/nirs/documents/final_out_ of_balance_report_april_2010.pdf>

14

PERMANENT DEBT BONDAGE FROM AMERICA'S STUDENT LOAN RACKET

For reasons good and bad, America in the 1950s differed markedly from today. Elected in 1952, Eisenhower was still president. Unemployment was low. Anyone wanting work found it. Most years the economy grew during a post-WW II expansion. Inflation was low. The average new car cost $1,500, a typical home under $10,000. College was affordable. Harvard's 1952 full year tuition was $600. Four years later it was $1,000—for a full, two-semester year. During the period, anyone could attend evenings at $5 a course and get a Harvard degree for about $175. Astonishing but true.

America was unchallenged economically, its manufacturing base offering high paying/good benefits jobs. Union representation was high. Southern and northern US cities were segregated. They still are, as 1960s civil rights gains have been lost, plus most good jobs and benefits. The additions of Alaska and Hawaii additions grew America to 50 states.

The Korean War left an unsettled armistice. Cold War politics settled in. Developing "mutually assured destruction (MAD)" and accommodation prevented WW III. Censure ruined Joe McCarthy, and by May 1957 he was dead at age 48. The CIA's first coup deposed Iran's Mohammad Mosaddegh. A generation of terror followed. A year later, another toppled Guatemala's Jacobo Arbenz Guzman, fueling decades of genocide against its indigenous peoples.

Throughout the decade, few followed Vietnam events, its defeat of France, and America's growing involvement in what became three decades of war. Palestinian territories weren't occupied, and during the period Israel was young, growing, but mostly out of the news and public mind.

Times indeed changed, for the worse, not better—including college tuition costs.

Harvard tuition for the 2010/2011 academic year is $35,568. Add room, board, health insurance fees, books and supplies, local transportation (if needed), plus miscellaneous and personal expenses and the total is nearly $60,000. Moreover, with annual tuition/fees hikes, incoming freshmen may need $70,000 or more for senior year expenses.

According to an October 28, 2010 *Los Angeles Times* article titled, "College costs increase faster than inflation:"

> State budget cuts and declines in philanthropy and endowments help push [college tuition costs] up much higher than general inflation across the country this year, amounting to an increase of 7.9% at public campuses and 4.5% at private ones, according to a new study by the nonprofit College Board.

In fact, some schools, like the University of California, raised fees by 32%, then announced a further 8% hike. The University of Illinois announced a 9.5% increase. Other public and private schools followed suit, some by over 10% at a time when fewer students can pay it. The College Board said for the decade ending in 2008, tuitions rose 54% after 49% in the previous decade. Expect more stiff hikes ahead.

Student Loans/Debt Information

The *Project Student Debt* website[1] has a wealth of information on student loans and debt. Using US Department of Education data for the 2007/08 academic year (the most recent available), it said two-thirds (or 1.4 million) of 2008 college graduates had student loan debt, a 27% increase from 2004, breaking down as follows:

- at public universities: 62%

- at private nonprofits: 72%

- at private for-profit institutions, 96% were debt entrapped.

In 2008, graduating seniors had an average debt burden of $23,200, a 24% increase from $18,650 in 2004. At public universities, it was $20,200. For private nonprofit ones, $27,650, and at private for-profit universities, $33,050.

However, given how government data is manipulated, true totals are far higher and rising exponentially. Many graduates have debt burdens approaching or exceeding $100,000. If repaid over 30 years, it amounts to a $500,000 obligation, and if in default, much more, because debt obligations aren't erased.

Moreover, regardless of inflation changes, tuition and fees rise annually. As a result, future costs are less affordable. Greater debt burdens are created, and for many students, higher education is out of reach.

For most others, completing college includes debt bondage because of what Valley Advocate.com writer Stephanie Kraft called "Killer Loans" in her October 14, 2010 article, saying:

> ...a large segment of the population is squeezed for interest payments and fees on loans taken out to pay for college, or for graduate or professional school.

The numbers are staggering—$96 billion loaned annually to attend college, graduate, trade or professional schools, excluding "shadow" borrowing. It includes tapping home equity, retirement accounts, other sources, and credit cards. A 2005 Smith College survey found 23% of students use plastic for college tuition and fees.

In the past decade, student loan debt ballooned over fourfold. In 1977, about $1.8 billion was borrowed. By 1989, it was $12 billion, and in 1996 $30 billion. According to the Student Loan Debt Clock, its cumulative principal and interest exceed $900 billion, surpassing credit card debt for the first time in June 2010, and expected to exceed $1 trillion in early 2012.

At its present rate, it increases $2,854 per second, entrapping most borrowers and forcing others to default. According to the *Chronicle of Higher Education* (CHE) in September 2010, "The percentage of borrowers defaulting on their student loans [rose] for a third year in a row, reaching an 11-year high of 7 percent," based on US Education Department data—again grossly understated to hide a serious problem for millions.

The data is based on the number of graduates defaulting within two years of graduation so it only captures "a sliver of the defaults that occur over the life of a loan," according to a CHE analysis. It estimates that one in five government loans entering repayment in 1995 defaulted. For community college graduates, it's 31% and at for-profit schools, 40%.

Yet little is reported on the scope of the student loan racket. The website *Student Loan Justice*[2] explains it, saying:

> The federal student loan system has become predatory due to the Congressional removal of standard consumer protections and...sanctioned collection powers that are stronger than those for all other loan instruments in our nation's history.

As a result, student borrowers are greatly harmed by unmanageable loan demands. Along with inflation and annual tuition/fee hikes, most graduates face an enormous burden, with no consumer protections, even in default. Once entrapped, escape is impossible. Debt bondage is permanent, and future lives and careers are impaired.

Congress ended bankruptcy protections, refinancing rights, statutes of limitations, truth in lending requirements, fair debt collection ones, and state usury laws when applied to federally guaranteed student loans. As a result, lenders may freely garnish wages, income tax refunds, earned income tax credits, and Social Security and disability income to assure defaulted loan payments. In addition, defaulting may cause loss of professional licenses, making repayment even harder or impossible.

Under a congressionally established default loan fee system, holders may keep 20% of all payments before any portion is applied to principal and interest due. A borrower's only recourse is to request an onerous and expensive "loan rehabilitation" procedure whereby they must make extended payments (not applied to principal or interest), then arrange a new loan for which additional fees are incurred. For many, permanent debt bondage is assured. The fact that there is no appeals process allowing a determination of default challenges lets lenders rip off borrowers, many in perpetuity.

> This fee system and associated rehabilitation schemes have provided a massive revenue stream for a shadowy nationwide network of politically connected [lenders], guarantors, servicers, and collection companies who have greatly enriched themselves at the expense of misfortunate borrowers.

As a result, millions of students and families have been gravely harmed, relegated to lifetime debt bondage. Yet industry predators thrive. The fee system is their "lifeblood," providing on average 60% of their income through "legalized wealth extraction"—a congressionally sanctioned extortion racket like Wall Street and unscrupulous investment companies scamming customers.

Lenders thrive from defaults, deriving income from debt service and inflated collection fees. A conspiratorial alliance of lenders, guarantors, servicers, collection companies, and government prey on unsuspecting borrowers. Lifetime default rates approach up to one third of undergraduate loans, higher than for subprime mortgages. "This, in fact, is higher than the default rate of any known [US] lending instrument..."

A Brief History of Federally Guaranteed Student Loans

In 1965, the Higher Education Act (HEA) let millions of students afford college with federally guaranteed loans and scholarships. It was later amended six times to benefit lenders at the expense of borrowers.

In 1978, the Bankruptcy Reform Act was the first comprehensive change since 1898. It established federal bankruptcy courts, substantially revamping former practices. It also made it easier to file, and prohibited discrimination when declared.

Bankruptcy discharges release debtors from personal liability for certain types of debt. In other words, debtors no longer must pay those debts, which are discharged permanently. Collection actions are also prohibited, although the debt remains. Bankruptcy doesn't eliminate it. Non-dischargeable debts, however, stay legally enforceable despite bankruptcy discharge. In 1990, the non-discharge period was extended to seven years.

In 1998, Congress eliminated federal Title IV, HEA student loan debt dischargeability in bankruptcy. Education loans are the only ones affected by a federal "no-escape" provision. In 2005, the Bankruptcy Abuse Prevention and Consumer Protection Act made all student loans (federal and private) non-dischargeable.

As a result, avoiding debt bondage by bankruptcy is impossible, unleashing the current predatory system for lenders like Sallie Mae. In 2009, the Department of Education reported over five million student loans in default. So are at least another one million private ones, and these numbers are way underestimated.

In addition, as explained above, prior protections were removed, including statute of limitations on collections, truth in lending, fair debt collection practices, the right to refinance, and state usury law prohibitions. Washington corrupted the system for lenders at the expense of student borrowers.

An Example of Systemic Predation

Sallie Mae (SM) is the largest student loan originator, servicer and collector, managing over $180 billion in federally guaranteed and private loans from over 10 million borrowers. If they can't be repaid after 270 days, the loans are in default. Washington pays SM the balance plus interest. For repayment, collection agencies like General Revenue Corporation (GRC), the nation's largest, impose 25% loan collection fees plus 28% commission charges on borrowers, and can garnish wages and other income for payment.

No statute of limitations applies. For GRC and other predators, a steady profit stream is assured at the expense of borrowers. Even schools benefit by raising tuition and fees far above inflation rates and income growth, making college more expensive, less affordable, while assuring higher future defaults on greater amounts.

Obama's student loan overhaul was a scam. Effective July 1, 2010, it does little to mitigate lenders' ability to rip off borrowers in perpetuity, yet he called it "one of the most significant investments in higher education since the GI bill." He lied.

The 1944 Servicemen's Readjustment Act (the GI Bill) covered most college or vocational training costs for 7.8 million returning vets plus a year of unemployment compensation. In addition, 2.4 million got VA-backed low-interest, no down payment home loans at a time their average cost was under $5,000, enabling millions of families to afford them, many with government help. In contrast, Obama's Student Aid and Fiscal Responsibility Act enriches providers, not borrowers, who are given chump change as usual.

Soaring Defaults During Hard Times

An April 21, 2009 *Wall Street Journal* article, "Student Loans: Default Rates are Soaring" by Anne Marie Chaker, highlighted the burden on students, saying the combination of economic weakness, rising tuitions and poor job prospects has caused defaults on student loans to skyrocket. According to Department of Education numbers for those federally guaranteed, estimated FY 2007 default rates reached 6.9%, up from 4.6% two years earlier.

Conditions are now far worse. Defaults "rose to 13.8% from 11.8% for students beginning repayment in (FY) 2008 compared with those starting a year earlier,"[3] according to new Department of Education data.

It measures defaults within the first three years of repayment. Over loan lifetimes, however, defaults approach two and a half times that level, perhaps heading for 50% if economic conditions keep deteriorating while tuition and fee rates rise.

Students at for-profit schools fare worst at 25%, but sharp tuition increases at public and private nonprofit universities place greater burdens on their graduates, assuring rising defaults, especially over their lifetime.

Moreover, rising levels may cause many colleges to become ineligible for government-backed Pell Grants and other student loans. To qualify formerly, they had to show less than 25% of students defaulting within a two year window. If they breach that threshold for three consecutive years, or hit 40% in a single year, they could lose out altogether. Now, under the 2008 Higher Education Opportunity Act increasing the default window to three years, the ineligibility threshold has risen to 30%, with penalties not beginning until 2014.

According to a new study conducted for the Institute for Higher Education Policy by Alisa Cunningham and Gregory Kienzl,[4] for every student defaulting, "at least two more fall behind in payments," It explains that around 40% of borrowers were delinquent within a five year repayment window. Almost one-fourth of them postponed payments to avoid delinquency. However, doing so made their interest and overall debt burden more onerous because escape is impossible.

Data from five of the country's largest student loan agencies showed only 37% of borrowers who began repayments in 2005 did so on time, a number now decreasing during hard times.

On April 11, 2011, *New York Times* writer Tamar Lewin headlined, "Burden of College Loans on Graduates Grows," saying:

> Two-thirds of bachelor's degree recipients graduated with debt in 2008, compared with less than half in 1993.

Rising debt burdens contribute to soaring default rates, especially for private for-profit universities. Moreover, given Pell Grant cuts and rising tuitions, students will be increasingly indebted and strapped to repay during hard times because Congress rigged the system against them.

As a result, education policy experts expect serious implications for future graduates. According to Lauren Asher, Institute for College Access and Success president:

> If you have a lot of people finishing or leaving school [entrapped in] debt, their choices may be very different than the generation before them. Things like buying a home, starting a family, starting a business, saving for their own kids' education may not be an option if they're trying to repay student debt.

Moreover, there's "much more awareness about student borrowing than there was 10 years ago. People either are in debt or know someone in debt."

Many of them have their own horror stories about how predatory lenders, servicers, guarantors, and collection companies rip them off under an escape-proof system. The entire scheme amounts to legalized grand theft, the equivalent of what Wall Street banks do to investors with impunity. According to Deanne Loonin, a National Consumer Law Center attorney:

> About two-thirds of the people I see attended for-profit [universities]. Most did not complete their program, and no one I have worked with has ever gotten a job in the field they were supposedly trained for. For them, the negative [debt default] mark on their credit report is the

No. 1 barrier to moving ahead in their lives. It doesn't just delay their ability to buy a house, it gets in the way of their employment prospects, finding an apartment, almost anything they try to do.

A Final Comment

More than ever, higher education is out of reach for millions. Most others require substantial scholarship and/or student loan help. During times of economic crisis, families are greatly burdened to assist financially. A 2008 National Center for Public Policy and Higher Education study said they contribute, on average, 55% of their income for public, four-year institutions, up from 39% in 2000, and higher still today to meet rising school costs.

As a result, today's higher education means crushing debt burdens at a time when systemic high unemployment and fewer good jobs make repaying them onerous to impossible. America's ownership society is heartless, favoring capital, not popular interests—a policy with strong bipartisan support.

Endnotes

1   Available at <http://www.projectonstudentdebt.org>
2   Available at <http://studentloanjustice.org/argument.htm>
3   Mary Pilon and Melissa Korn, "Student-Loan Default Rates Worsen", *Wall Street Journal*, February 4, 2011.
4   Tamar Lewin, "Loan Study on Students Goes Beyond Default Rates," *The New York Times*, March 15, 2011, available at <http://www.ihep.org/assets/files/publications/a-f/Delinquency-The_Untold_Story_FINAL_March_2011.pdf>

15

ON THE CHOPPING BLOCK

SOCIAL SECURITY, MEDICARE, MEDICAID AND PUBLIC PENSIONS

Death by a thousand cuts—a.k.a. "creeping normalcy," making major changes seem normal by having them happen slowly, incrementally, like boiling a frog unaware it's dinner until cooked—that's what's in store. Social Security, Medicare and public pensions are dinner.

Yet both are insurance, not welfare, programs funded by worker-employer payroll tax deductions. They're contractual federal obligations to eligible recipients who qualify. However, you'd never know it by the way both programs are publicly discussed, with everything explained but the truth. More on that below.

On August 14, 1935, the Social Security Act became law. Known as the federal Old-Age, Survivors, and Disability Insurance program (OASDI), it provides retirement, disability, survivorship, and death benefits. It's still America's most effective poverty reduction program that's worked remarkably well since inception. It exists to provide secure inflation-adjusted retirement or disability income, unlike risking personal savings to create private wealth that may end up losing them.

Despite bogus claims, it's not going bankrupt. When properly administered, it's sound and secure, needing only modest adjustments at times to assure it.

On July 30, 1965, Lyndon Johnson signed the Social Security (Medicare) Act into law, enrolling Harry and Bess Truman as its first recipients.

Medicare.gov calls it "the nation's largest health insurance program," covering 40 million Americans. It's a "Health Insurance program for people age 65 or older, some disabled people under age 65, and people of all ages with End-Stage Renal Disease (permanent kidney failure treated with dialysis or a transplant)."

America's aristocracy wants Medicare and Social Security ended, citing the nation's burgeoning debt and enormous unfunded liabilities for both programs. The website *usdebtclock.org* lists them as follows:

1. the US National Debt: nearly $15 trillion;
2. Social Security Liability: over $15 trillion;
3. Prescription Drug Liability: over $20 trillion; and
4. Medicare Liability: over $79 trillion.
Total: nearly $114 trillion plus the National Debt.

Most importantly, future liabilities mask today's soundness that can remain sound if current programs are properly administered. That possibility is omitted from hyped scare tactics to convince future recipients to make unjustifiable sacrifices. Like it or not, however, the end is coming, as major media reports are promoting the idea as well as politicians from both parties.

On August 9, 2010, for example, a *New York Times* editorial headlined, "The Latest on Medicare and Social Security," saying:

Of course, neither program is sound for the long run. [Yet there's] time for lawmakers to reform and strengthen both [for] the long haul. [What's required is] a combination of benefits cuts and tax increases, which could be distributed fairly and phased in over decades.

An earlier May 13, 2009 *Wall Street Journal* report headlined "Social Security, Medicare Face Insolvency Sooner," said Medicare "will be depleted by 2017," Social Security by "2037."

In fact, neither program is endangered, as explained earlier. Yet the report continued:

Any attempt to address long-term fiscal problems will require big changes to the way entitlements are funded or paid out.

False, but don't expect major media reports to explain or side with recipients about programs too important to be weakened or lost.

In his January 2010 State of the Union address, Obama announced plans to "freeze government spending for three years," starting in 2011, saying he'd form a bipartisan fiscal commission to cut the deficit and tackle entitlements by imposed austerity at a time massive stimulus is needed.

Called the National Commission on Fiscal Responsibility and Reform (NCFRF), the "bipartisan fiscal commission" was co-chaired by two deficit hawks, former Senator Alan Simpson (R. WY) and Erskine Bowles, former Clinton White House Chief of Staff. They headed an 18-member team, stacked with like-minded ideologues, elitists knowing their own futures are secure.

Their mandate: slash Medicare, Medicaid, Social Security and other social spending, continuing a decades long process of transferring wealth to America's super-rich. On November 10, 2010, they issued their proposal.

Their recommendations included:

- ending or capping middle class tax breaks, including deductions for home mortgage insurance and tax-free employer provided medical insurance;

- lowering income taxes dramatically to 9, 15 and 24%, down from six brackets ranging from 10 - 35%;

- slashing corporate tax rates from the top 35% to 26%;

- making deep Medicare cuts as well as increasing Medicaid co-pays; and

- raising the Social Security retirement age to 69 by 2075, as well as reducing annual cost-of-living increases.

A second Bipartisan Policy Center (BPC) commission co-chaired by former Senator Pete Domenici (R. NM) and Alice Rivlin, former director of the Office of Management and Budget and the Congressional Budget Office, issued its own proposal called "Restoring America's Future."

Its recommendations include:

- indexing Social Security benefits to life expectancy to reduce them as longevity increases;

- eliminating annual cost-of-living adjustments, bogusly claiming inflation is overstated, especially for retirees facing costly medical expenses;

- instituting a one-year payroll tax holiday for workers and employers to save $650 billion, supposedly to be replenished from future general revenues, which in fact is a way to help kill Social Security as discussed below;

- sharply cutting Medicare and Medicaid benefits;

- simplifying the tax code to two brackets (15 and 27%), favoring the rich;

- eliminating home mortgage and most other deductions and credits;

- taxing employer provided health insurance; and

- instituting a 6.5% national sales tax, hitting ordinary people hardest.

Chapter 7 also addressed this, providing additional details.

Looting the So-Called "Trust Fund"

In March 2011, economist Paul Craig Roberts headlined his article, "The Greatest Rip-Off," explaining what Obama and right-wing ideologues conceal—namely that "[a]ccording to the official 2010 Social Security reports between 1984 and 2009, the American people contributed $2 trillion.... more to Social Security and Medicare in payroll taxes than was paid out in benefits." Including accumulated interest, it's $2.8 trillion.

Where did it go? Washington spent it "to finance wars and pork-barrel projects," putting a lie to the so-called "trust fund" that's all rhetoric, not reality. Moreover, depending on population and income growth plus other factors, OASDI (Old-Age Survivors, and Disability Insurance) will have produced surplus revenues of $31.6 trillion by 2085. In other words, the system is eminently solvent and then some, but public discussion won't explain it. Instead, right-wing ideologues want the program ended, bogusly saying it's going broke.

Social Security Works

Nancy Altman is co-director of Social Security Works (strengthensocialsecurity.org), an "American coalition (representing over 50 million Americans) united around the simple proposition, "Strengthen Social Security...Don't Cut It."

Its seven principles include:

1. Social Security didn't cause the federal deficit; it shouldn't be cut to reduce it.

2. It shouldn't be privatized.

3. It shouldn't be means-tested.

4. Future revenues should come by raising the payroll tax ceiling, requiring those earning more to pay their fair share.

5. The retirement age shouldn't increase further.

(6) Benefits shouldn't be cut, including by reducing annual infla-tion-adjusted increases.
(7) Benefits "should be increased for those who are most disadvan-taged."

In short, Social Security (Medicare and Medicaid) should be strengthened to provide greater, not lower, future benefits.

Obama's Destructive Payroll Tax Holiday

The proposed 2% worker payroll tax cut for one year is in actuality not a tax holiday but a stealth indefinite extension scheme to drain hundreds of billions of dollars from the Social Security Trust Fund. Doing so will irreparably weaken its ability to pay future benefits, the idea being to destroy it altogether, perhaps first by privatizing it.

Social Security Works explained how the tax holiday "could unravel" the whole system as follows:

1. "It's easy to enact tax cuts—It's very hard to end them."

2. Doing so results in a substantial tax increase—$2,000 on $100,000 a year earners, $400 for those making $20,000.

3. "Restoring the 2% lost....would be a nearly 50% tax increase (for) 94% of all Americans...."

4. House and Senate Republicans oppose any increases in taxes. So do many Democrats, especially in election years or when economic conditions are weak.

5. Obama's proposal undermines Social Security's long-term sol-vency. Repaying what's lost from general revenues is greatly im-peded by the size of the deficit and planned austerity coming to reduce it.

6. Maintaining the 2% cut indefinitely will cause massive benefit cuts and eliminate any chance for improving them, notably for so-ciety's poor and disadvantaged.

7. Middle class households will also be harmed, violating Franklin Roosevelt's pledge that:

We put those payroll contributions there so as to give the contributors a legal, moral, and political right to collect their pensions and their unemployment benefits. With those taxes in there, no damn politician can ever scrap my social security program. Those taxes aren't a matter of economics, they're straight politics.

FDR never met Obama or congressional Republicans and Democrats. What he gave, they'll end, violating a government-mandated right.

8. A payroll tax holiday is another step toward privatization, a sure way to kill Social Security, the way 401(k)s destroyed private pensions, leaving workers at the mercy of marketplace uncertainties that can wipe out life savings during hard times.

Social Security Works concluded by saying:

There are better ways to provide stimulus to the economy—and that do less harm to Social Security—than a tax holiday.

According to the Center for Budget and Policy Priorities (CBPP), one way is by extending the 2009 Making Work Pay Tax Credit, adding much more stimulus than a payroll tax holiday. It gives workers a refundable tax *credit*, increasing the size of the paychecks. At 6.2% of earned income, it provides maximum $400 for working individuals, $800 for married taxpayers filing joint returns.

A payroll tax holiday is a bad idea any time, besides doing little to stimulate economic growth. "The most efficient way to boost consumer spending is to put money into the hands of people who will spend it quickly rather than save it."

A payroll tax holiday does not score well on this front—too little of the benefit goes to lower-income households struggling to make ends meet and too much goes to higher-income taxpayers, who are likely to save a significant portion of any new resources they receive.

Besides killing Social Security, it also, as intended, transfers more wealth to the rich, which Republicans and Democrats, including Obama, endorse.

In contrast, the Making Work Pay Tax Credit poses no threat to Social Security. The payroll tax holiday may destroy it. Republicans signing on as a concession mask their real intent, the same one they've had since Social Security's enactment, a program they strongly opposed, as well as Medicare, in 1965. Now both parties oppose both.

Obama's payroll tax holiday will drive a stake into Social Security's heart, or as Hall of Fame former baseball announcer Bob Prince used to call Pittsburgh Pirate home runs: "Kiss it goodbye." Fans cheered.

Deathly silence will greet Obama's proposal once recipients know they've been scammed. Republicans and Democrats plan it unless an aroused public stops them.

Targeting Public Pensions

Budget-strapped states face major pressures to reduce or eliminate their public pension obligations, though doing so isn't easy under contractually binding contracts with employees. Nothing, however, prohibits them from switching from defined benefit to defined contribution plans like 401(k)s. In fact, it's what most corporations did years earlier at the expense of assured retirement benefits.

Congress is also targeting federal pensions that civilian employees receive under the Federal Employees Retirement System (FERS), consisting of three components:

- a FERS annuity defined benefit plan;

- mandatory Social Security participation; however, most Civil Service Retirement System (CSRS) employees aren't part of Social Security unless they qualify separately from additional private sector employment, and

- the Thrift Savings Plan (TSP), a 401(k) type defined contribution plan.

On March 19, 2011, Senators Tom Coburn (R. OK) and Richard Burr (R. NC) introduced S. 644: Public-Private Employee Retirement Parity Act to prohibit federal annuities for employees hired after 2012. In other words, beginning January 1, 2013, they want defined pensions for newly hired federal workers ended, eventually eliminating unfunded ones altogether.

Although the other two FERS components are maintained, S. 644 is another step toward halting all federal obligations to working Americans in order to make more funds available for imperial wars, corporate handouts, and greater tax benefits for America's super-rich. But don't expect Congress, Obama, or major media reports to explain.

Coburn justified S. 644 by claiming federal workers earn over 20% more than private sector ones. In fact, according to a National Institute on Retirement Security (NIRS) study titled, "Out of Balance? Comparing Public and Private Sector Compensation Over 20 Years",[1] wages and benefits combined for public workers are lower than for private sector ones "with comparable earnings determinants," such as education and work experience. Moreover, the pay gap widened over the last 15 years. Other studies agree, saying public workers can earn more by using their skills in private sector jobs.

As a result, the National Federation of Federal Employees (NFFE) called S. 644 unfair. For example, a federal employee earning on average $50,000 in his or her three highest earning years, with 30 years of service, gets a $15,000 annual pension, hardly a generous amount.

NFFE also said FERS pensions are less than under the Civil Service Retirement System (CSRS), the one FERS replaced in 1986 for new hires.

Coburn and Burr claim defined benefit federal pensions are going broke. In September 2010, in fact, the Congressional Research Service (CRS) denied insolvency problems, saying FERS and CSRS (for eligible employees) will be able to meet their obligations "in perpetuity." Moreover, CRS expects their assets to grow for decades, reaching $15.3 trillion in 2080, far exceeding outlays.

Nonetheless, congressional Republicans, known as "You Cutters," plan other slash and burn efforts to:

- cut federal pay;

- freeze hiring;

- end early retirement benefits;

- eliminate the time the American Federation of Government Employees (AFGE) has to defend federal employee rights; and

- calculate pensions based on the highest five (instead of 3) working years, among other proposed draconian anti-worker measures, including stealing pension funds by borrowing them to fund government operations.

On May 16, *Washington Post* writer Zachary Goldfarb headlined, "Treasury to tap pensions to help fund government,"[2] saying that federal retirement funds will be tapped to help fund government operations after the $14.3 trillion debt ceiling was reached as Congress keeps wrangling over raising it. In fact:

> the Obama administration has shown growing interest in altering [pension] programs to curb the debt in the long run [by] raising the amount that federal employees contribute to their pensions.

> Both parties agree on social spending cuts overall, disagreeing

largely on the timing ahead of the 2012 election, leaving both sides posturing for political advantage. In fact, Obama has already committed to cutting trillions of dollars over the next decade, mainly essential entitlements, education, healthcare for working households, and aid to America's poor.

In addition, federal workers' pay was frozen in November 2010 for two years, despite greater inflationary pressures than reported—as anyone who eats, drives a car, heats a home, pays medical bills, or defrays college tuition costs knows.

But there's more going on as well under a little recognized federal regulatory scheme to seize 401(k) retirement funds. On February 26, 2011, a White House Office of the Vice President press release headlined, "Vice President Biden Issues Middle Class Task Force Annual Report."[3]

Chapter 3 calls for enhancing middle class "retirement options [through] new regulations to improve the transparency and adequacy of 401(k) retirement savings" under so-called "Guaranteed Retirement Accounts (GRAs)," explained disingenuously as follows:

> Some have suggested the creation of [GRAs], which would give workers a simple way to invest a portion of their retirement savings in an account that was free of inflation and market risk, and in some versions under discussion, would guarantee a specified real return above the rate of inflation.

In fact, if enacted, GRAs will be federally controlled to be borrowed from, exploited, or otherwise used at the whim of government authorities, perhaps as a first step toward seizing them or reducing their value in ways similar to how Wall Street manipulates markets.

Overall, bipartisan support endorses ending safety net protections, especially Social Security, Medicare, Medicaid, and public pensions, forcing Americans to pay more and get less if anything at all.

At the same time as Biden's report was released, the White House, together with the Treasury and Labor Departments, issued a so-called "Request for Information," calling for analyzing the pros and cons of annuitizing 401(k)s. The idea had already been discussed on February 2, 2010 in suggested Federal Register "Proposed Rules," which stated:

> While defined contribution plans have some strengths relative to defined benefit plans, participants in defined contributions plans bear the investment risk because there is no promise by the employer as to the adequacy of the account balance that will be available or the income stream that can be provided in retirement.[4]

As a result, federal agaencies "are considering whether it would be appropriate for them to take future steps for them to facilitate access to, and use of, lifetime income or other arrangements designed to provide a stream of income after retirement."[5]

Though no action so far has been taken, federal officials even threaten personal savings if measures like the above schemes are adopted.

A Final Comment

On April 15, the majority controlled House passed H. Con. Res. 34: Establishing the budget for the United States for fiscal year 2012 through 2021. It was a symbolic vote to end Medicare and Medicaid, as well as reward US corporations and America's aristocracy with another $3 trillion in handouts.

Though not legally binding or likely to be passed by the Senate, it highlights this chapter's theme. With bipartisan support, future measures will destroy hard-won benefits, essential entitlements without which millions will lose affordable healthcare and be plunged into poverty and despair, forced to wage imperial wars and transfer maximum wealth to US elites, which has been an ongoing process for the last three decades.

In fact, repeated House and Senate actions under Democrat and Republican leadership redefine chutzpah and irresponsible governance, revealing their own illegitimacy in the process.

Endnotes

1   Available at <http://www.nirsonline.org/index.php?option=com_content&task=view&id=395&Itemid=48>

2   Available at <http://www.washingtonpost.com/business/economy/treasury-to-tap-pensions-to-help-fund-government/2011/05/15/AF2fqK4G_story.html?hpid=z2>

3   Available at <http://webcache.googleusercontent.com/search?q=cache:Yufov X2AR2YJ:www.whitehouse.gov/the-press-office/vice-president-biden-issues-middle-class-task-force-annual-report+biden's+february+2011+annual+report+on+the+middle+class&cd=1&hl=en&ct=clnk&gl=us&client=safari&source=www.google.com>

4   Available at <http://edocket.access.gpo.gov/2010/pdf/2010-2028.pdf>

5   Id.

16

THE FEDERAL RESERVE ABOLITION ACT

Since 1999, Ron Paul has introduced the Federal Reserve Abolition Act (FRAA) numerous times. No further action has been taken. The legislation was referred to the House Committee on Financial Services, ignored, and effectively killed.

FRAA is a bold, needed measure to "abolish the Board of Governors of the Federal Reserve System and the Federal reserve banks, to repeal the Federal Reserve Act, and for other purposes."

It provides for management of employees, assets and liabilities of the Board during a dissolution period, and designates the Director of the Office of Management and Budget to:

- liquidate Fed assets in an orderly and expeditious manner;

- transfer them to the General Fund of the Treasury after satisfying all claims against the Board and any Federal Reserve bank;

- assume all outstanding Board and member bank liabilities and transfer them to the Secretary of the Treasury; and

- after an 18-month period, submit a report to Congress "containing a detailed description of the actions taken to implement this Act and any actions or issues relating to such implementation that remain uncompleted or unresolved as of the date of the report."

On November 22, 2007, "End the Fed" protests were held in dozens of cities nationwide (including New York, Chicago, Los Angeles and Washington, DC), but you'd hardly know it for lack of coverage. Attendee demands were simple and straightforward:

- end a private banking cartel's illegal monopoly of the nation's

161

money supply and price (short funds interest rate);

- return that power to the US Treasury as the Constitution mandates;

- end a fiat currency system backed by the full faith and credit of the government; and

- return America to a sound, hard currency monetary system.

"End the Fed! Sound Money for America!" is what people want, writer and US policy critic Webster Tarpley noted, saying:

> ....the privately owned central bank....has been looting and wrecking the US economy for almost a hundred years. We must end a system where unelected, unaccountable cliques of bankers and financiers loyal to names like Morgan, Rockefeller, and Mellon set interest rates and money supply behind closed doors, leading to de-industrialization, mass impoverishment, and a world economic and financial depression of incalculable severity.

In theory, the Fed was established to stabilize the economy, smooth out the business cycle, manage healthy, sustainable growth, and maintain stable prices. In fact, it failed dismally. It contributed to 19 US recessions (including the Great Depression) and significantly to the following equity market declines accompanying them as measured by the Dow or S & P 500 average:

- 40.1% (Dow) from 1916-1917;

- 46.6% (Dow) from 1919- 1921;

- the 1929 (Dow) crash in two stages—47.9% in 1929 followed by a strong, temporary rebound; then 86%; an 89% peak to trough total from October 1929 to July 1932;

- 49.1% (Dow) from 1937-1938;

- 40.4% (Dow) from 1939-1942;

- 25.3% (S & P) from 1946-1947;

- 19.8% (S & P) in 1957;

- 26.8% (S & P) from 1961-1962;

- 19.3% (S & P) in 1966;

- 32.7% (S & P) from 1968-1970;

- 45.1% (S & P) from 1973-1974;

- 20.2% (S & P) from 1980-1982;

- 32.9% (S & P) in 1987;

- 19.2% (S & P) in 1990;

- 18.8% (S & P) in 1998;

- 49.1% (S & P) from 2000-2002; and

- over 57% (S & P) from October 2007-March 2009.

The Fed also caused monetary inflation and the decline of America's standard of living since its 1913 inception, especially since the 1970s. From the late 18th century to 1913, virtually no inflation existed under the gold standard except during times of war. Using government data, it now takes over $2000 to equal $100 of pre-Fed purchasing power. In other words, a 1913 dollar is worth less than a nickel today.

At that time, a dollar was defined as 1/20 of an ounce of gold or about an ounce of silver. The Fed then changed the standard away from precious metals to the full faith and credit of the government. Ever since (except during the 1930s and WW II price controls) inflation eroded the currency's value to where it stands at this day.

It's why one analyst calls the dollar "nothing more than a popular symbol for the tangible substances it once represented—gold and silver." Its declining value represents waning world confidence in America's ability to repay debt obligations, with good reason.

Under the Federal Reserve System (besides inflation), we've had:

- rising consumer debt;

- record budget and trade deficits;

- a soaring national debt;

- a high level of personal and business bankruptcies;

- currently, millions of home foreclosures;

- high unemployment;

- loss of the nation's manufacturing base;

- growing millions in poverty;

- an unprecedented wealth gap; and

- a hugely unstable economy lurching from one crisis to another.

Easy money, market manipulation, deregulation, reckless specula-tion, counterproductive fixes, and unsustainable debt caused today's crisis. Why else would gold and silver prices soar? Bad policy assures worse trou-ble ahead. Instead of excesses being washed out, they increase over time, heading for an eventual house of cards collapse.

Abolish the Fed and Return Money Creation Power to Congress Where It Belongs

Ron Paul led the effort for years, saying on the House floor on September 10, 2002:

> Since the creation of the Federal Reserve, middle and working-class Americans have been victimized by a boom-and-bust monetary policy. In addition, most Americans have suffered a steadily eroding purchasing power because of the Federal Reserve's inflationary policies. This represents a real, if hidden, tax imposed on the American people...
>
> It is time for the Congress to put the interests of the American people ahead of the special interests. Abolishing the Federal Reserve will allow Congress to reassert its constitutional authority over monetary policy.
>
> Abolishing the Federal Reserve and returning to a constitutional system [as mandated] will enable America to return to the type of monetary system envisioned by our nation's founders: one where the value of money is consistent because it is tied to a commodity such as gold....I urge my colleagues [to co-sponsor] my legislation to abolish the Federal Reserve.

Paul regularly introduced his legislation. Each time, it died in committee. On November 22, 2007, he attended the End the Fed rally in Houston, addressed the crowd, and called the current economic crisis as bad or worse than the 1930s, saying, "we know who caused it. It was the

Federal Reserve that gave us all this trouble," explaining that America had a "free ride for decades because we've had a system that was devised where the dollar could act as if it were gold."

But it wasn't—not after Nixon closed the gold window in August 1971, ending the 1944 Bretton Woods Agreement, no longer letting dollars be backed by gold or converted to it in international markets. A "new economic system" was created, letting Washington "spend beyond our means, live beyond our means, [and] print money beyond our means," causing past and current crises.

America created "an appearance of great wealth. But it was doomed to fail," and that became apparent since fall 2007 heralded "the failure of the dollar reserve standard that was set up in August of 1971. It has ended. The only question" is what will replace it?

Some suggest a new international fiat currency. Nations embracing it, however, would be surrendering their sovereignty to a higher authority. It's vital to halt efforts for one world government and a global currency. If not, America's Constitution will be subverted. When written, it gave Congress exclusive money creation power. Article I, Section 8 gives it the right to coin (create) money and regulate the value thereof. The founders also wanted gold and silver to be legal tender, not fiat money, nor should a privately controlled central bank exist.

In 1935, the Supreme Court ruled that Congress cannot constitutionally delegate that power to another body. By creating the Federal Reserve System in 1913, Congress violated its sworn mandate to uphold and defend the Constitution. The US public was defrauded. Today's crisis is the fruit of bad policy.

But watch out.

"The writing is on the wall, and the end of this system" approaches. "They cannot patch it up, they can't up it back together again. They know it and we know it. The only argument is what is it going to be replaced with?"[1]

"Central banks in the West especially [had] been dumping gold to artificially lower [its price] to pretend the dollar is of great value." They did it until prices reversed and soared, reflecting what Daniel Webster once said: "There can be no legal tender in this country....but gold and silver. This is a constitutional principle....of the very highest importance."

Gold, however, wasn't the original monetary system standard. Silver was, the silver dollar, and only a constitutional amendment can change it.

Moreover, paper currency, whether or not backed by gold, wasn't hard money the Constitution authorized. Honest money is gold and silver weights and measures. Federal Reserve Notes are fiat debt obligations, representing a mechanism of wealth transference from the public to a privileged elite—through inflation and loss of purchasing power. It enriches few, leaving many indebted, especially under privatized banking control.

America's monetary system combines money, credit and debt into a dishonest system of empty promises in exchange for future ones. There's no eventual payment, only a new generation of obligations to repay what earlier ones accumulated.

It's a moneychangers dream—ever-expanding debt and a continuing interest rate stream, masquerading as popular wealth creation. In fact, it's systemic debt bondage, benefitting the few at the expense of many, modern-day neofeudalism. This is how an elite 1% amassed 70% of the nation's wealth.

In the 1920s, Josiah Stamp, Bank of England president, said:

> Banking was conceived in iniquity and was born in sin. Bankers own the earth. Take it away from them, but leave them the power to create deposits, and with a flick of the pen [today a computer keyboard] they will create enough deposits to buy it back again. However, take it away from them, and all the great fortunes like mine will disappear, and they ought to disappear, for this would be a happier and better world to live in. But if you wish to remain the slaves of Bankers and pay the cost of your own slavery, let them continue to create deposits.

Creating the Federal Reserve System let bankers, not government, control the price and amount of fiat money, the root cause of today's crisis. Returning money creation power to Congress, along with public banks replacing private ones, represents the best hope for restoring and sustaining economic stability and growth.

The Free Lakotah Bank

On November 24, 2008 the following press release announced: "People of Lakota Launch Private Bank for Only Silver and Gold Currencies." All deposits are

> liquid, meaning they can be withdrawn at any time in minted rounds. Some may confuse our economic system with isolationism....which it is not. Since we currently produce much more than we consume, we have the right to decide what medium of exchange to accept for our effort. And so we accept only value for value. Across our great land, over thousands of tribes and merchants

participate in our system of trade. We invite others to trade with us and bring value back into our transactions.

It's the world's first non-reserve, non-fractional bank that accepts only silver and gold currencies for deposit. The Lakotas

invite people of any creed, faith or heritage to unite in an effort to reclaim control of wealth. It is our hope that other tribal nations and American citizens recognize the importance of silver and gold as currency and decide to mirror our system of honest trade.

The bank states that it issues, circulates and accepts for deposit "only AOCS—Approved silver and gold currencies." It calls paper not real money but "merely a promise to pay—a mortgage on wealth that does not exist, backed by a gun aimed at those who are expected to produce it. Since we deal only in real money, we do not participate in any central bank looting schemes." When corruption is rewarded and "honesty becom[es] self-sacrifice....you may know that your society is doomed."

As longtime victims of adversity,[2] Lakotas are working to prevent it.

However, if public, not private, banks controlled America's money, fiat paper would be as good as gold or at least close, because inflation could be eliminated or greatly reduced.

End the Fed

Privatized money control is the single greatest threat to democracy and sustainable economic stability and growth. The two are incompatible as former lawyer, economist, academic, and Canadian Prime Minister (from 1935-1948) William Lyon Mackenzie King once said:

Until the control of the issue of currency and credit is restored to government and recognized as its most conspicuous and sacred responsibility, all talk of sovereignty of Parliament and of democracy is idle and futile....Once a nation parts with control of its credit, it matters not who makes (its) laws....Usury once in control will wreck any nation..."

and indeed it has, far more now than ever.

It worried Thomas Jefferson enough to call banking institutions "more dangerous to our liberties than standing armies" at a much simpler time in US history.

The right to create and control money belongs to the people through their elected representatives. For nearly a century, unaccountable powerful bankers usurped it. They effectively run the country and own it. Unless public pressure redeems it, political tyranny will follow privately controlled money power, stealing public wealth until America's aristocracy gets it all.

Endnotes

1   "Ron Paul: End the Fed", *RonPaul.com*, November 23, 2008, available at <http://www.ronpaul.com/2008-11-23/ron-paul-end-the-fed/>

2   My earlier discussion on how America treated indigenous Lakotahs is available at <http://sjlendman.blogspot.com/2008/11/fate-of-lakotahs-highlights-americas.html>

17

PUBLIC BANKING

AN IDEA WHOSE TIME
HAS COME

The 1913 Federal Reserve Act let powerful bankers usurp America's money system in violation of the Constitution's Article I, Section 8, giving only Congress the power to "coin Money [and] regulate the Value thereof..." Thereafter, powerful bankers victimized working Americans, using money, credit and debt for private self-enrichment by bankrolling and colluding with Congress and successive administrations to implement laws favoring themselves.

As a result, decades of deregulation, outsourcing, economic financialization, and casino capitalism followed, eroding purchasing power, producing asset bubbles, record budget and national debt levels, and depression-sized unemployment far higher than reported numbers, which aremanipulated to look better.

After the financial crisis erupted in late 2007, harder than ever Main Street hard times followed, and it's getting worse, not better. High levels of personal and business bankruptcies have resulted. Millions of homes have been lost. Record numbers of Americans are newly impoverished. An unprecedented wealth gap is steadily growing. America's unstable economy lurches from one crisis to another. The current one miring Main Street in depression, is still in its early stages.

Recovery is pure illusion. Today's contagion has spread out of control globally. No one's sure how to contain it, though Wall Street got trillions of dollars in a desperate attempt to socialize losses, privatize profits, and pump life back into a corpse.

Speculation and debt need more of the same to prosper, but ultimately it's a losing game. The greater the expansion, the harder it falls, especially when credit contraction persists. Job creation is moribund. Industrial America keeps imploding. High-paying jobs are exported. Economic prospects are eroding. Workers are exploited for greater corporate profits, and no one's sure how to revive stable, sustainable long-term growth.

Privatized money control is the primary problem, representing democracy's greatest threat. Regaining public control can restore the American economy. The time for launching public banking across America is now, when more than ever, it's needed.

Cause and Effect

Economist Michael Hudson explains that "debt leveraging" caused America's economic collapse, so piling on more exacerbates conditions, especially in the way it's done, by:

- bailing out giant Wall Street banks;

- letting them used trillions in public funds for more speculation, big bonuses, and acquisitions, rather than for direct lending to revive growth;

- not acting as a lender of last resort to facilitate private investment to create jobs, turn around a sick economy, and stimulate demand; and

- letting federal debt unproductively skyrocket to stratospheric levels, affirming Adam Smith's dictum that no country ever repaid their debts, especially the kind banking cartels create in lieu of workable alternatives not taken.

Key among them is:

- nationalizing the Fed, returning money creation power to Congress;

- abolishing Wall Street's franchise;

- breaking up giant banks;

- liquidating insolvent too-big-to-fail ones; and

- replacing them with publicly run banks, providing low-interest loans to businesses, farmers, communities, households, students, and other worthy borrowers as a way to revive and sustain inflation-free prosperity.

It's no pipe dream. It's real. This has happened before in the United States and can again. Short of that, according to Hudson:

debt service will [keep] crowd[ing] out spending on goods

and services and there will be no recovery. Debt deflation will drag the economy down while assets are transferred further into the hands of the wealthiest 10% of the population [mainly the top 1%], operating via the financial sector.[1]

Eventually the economy will collapse, but not Wall Street, which is profiting hugely with public handouts—aided and abetted by corrupted public officials, who are turning America into what Hudson calls a "zombie economy" and banana republic.

Workable Alternatives Can Prevent Economic Collapse

Ellen Brown's extraordinary book titled *Web of Debt* explains how private money power trapped Americans in debt and how they can break free. At issue is private v. publicly created credit. Brown says:

Readily available credit made America 'the land of opportunity' ever since the days of the American colonists. What transformed this credit system into a Ponzi scheme, that must continually be propped up with bailout money, is that the credit power has been turned over to private bankers who always require more money back than they create...[2]

Indeed, private bankers require *much more* money back than they create. In contrast, when federal, state or local governments lend their own money, profit isn't at issue so rates can be low and affordable to businesses, farmers, and private individuals. Moreover, for federal and municipality needs, government-issued credit is interest-free. In fact, it's a primary way of maintaining or increasing the money supply—putting money directly to work financing public needs.

Brown explained that "fractional reserve banking" dates from the 17th century, done then mainly in gold and silver coins. Early bankers soon realized it was simpler to use deposit receipts (called notes) as a means of payment so they began creating money by making loans through promises to pay. More could be issued than the amount of coins on hand as only enough were needed to service redemptions—today's idea of a reserve requirement.

What began earlier as notes, today are accounting entries that literally create money out of thin air. Moreover, the process would and has worked the same for government as for privately-owned banks, except as publicly-run institutions, their mandate greatly differs:

- They don't have to earn profits.

- They're not beholden to Wall Street or shareholders.

- Only the state, community, (or federal government's) credit-worthiness matters. So far, in over 230 years, no state ever went out of business, and, except for Arkansas during the Great Depression, none ever defaulted, even when poorly governed.

Further, they can lend to themselves and municipalities interest-free, as well as to businesses, farmers, and individuals at low affordable rates to create sustainable, inflation-free growth. Moreover, the more often loans roll over, the more debt-free money is created—inflation-free, if used productively for growth rather than for speculation, big bonuses and other excesses.

In fact, as long as new money produces goods and services, inflation can't occur. Only imbalances cause problems— "when 'demand' (money) exceeds 'supply' (goods and services)." Price stability is assured when both increase proportionally, and that's exactly how it worked in colonial America and under Lincoln during the Civil War.

Brown's *Web of Debt* provided several examples of what works best:

- In colonial America, government money creation worked impressively, first in Massachusetts in 1691 which put out its own paper money called scrip, backed by the government's full faith and credit. Other colonies followed, freeing themselves from British banks, letting their economies prosper, inflation-free, with no taxation for 25 years, paying no interest to bankers.

- Lincoln did the same thing with government-created money, interest free. What followed turned America into an industrial giant by launching the steel industry, a continental railroad system, and a new era of farm machinery and cheap tools. Free education was also established. The Homestead Act gave settlers ownership rights and encouraged land development. Government supported science. Mass production methods were standardized. Labor productivity rose exponentially during America's greatest growth period before the Fed's 1913 creation changed everything.

- The Middle Ages, falsely portrayed as a backward and impoverishing era saved only by industrial capitalism, in fact, under its banker-free tally system, prospered for hundreds of years.

- Early 20th century Australia under its publicly-run Commonwealth Bank, created money, made loans, and collected interest at a fraction of what private bankers charge. It worked well enough, in fact, for the country to have one of the highest global living standards at the time. It showed the benefits that were possible through government created credit compared to privatized banking power's destructiveness. However, once private bankers took over, Australia became heavily indebted, and its living standard fell precipitously.

- China enjoyed a banker-free system for thousands of years before privatized banking, and today Beijing directs The People's Bank of China (its semi-independent central bank) to grow the nation's economy and create millions of jobs for its burgeoning population.

- Venezuela, under its public service mandated a quasi-public/private system, offers a far more stable/responsible system than America's predatory Fed-run one. See below for more on Venezuelan banking.

Imagine the possibilities under public banks:

- Federal, state and local debt could be substantially reduced or eliminated.

- So could personal and payroll federal taxes.

- America's manufacturing base could be rebuilt.

- Social programs could be funded inflation-free.

- Vital infrastructure projects could be undertaken on a scale never before imagined, including cleaning up the environment and developing alternate, sustainable, clean, safe, affordable energy sources.

- Millions of new well-paying jobs could be created, ending unemployment for everyone able to work; and for those willing but unable, aid could be provided.

- Foreclosures would end, and the dream of home ownership would be reachable for everyone because mortgages would be plentiful, cheap, and not designed to scam the unwary.

- Booms and busts would end.

- Destructive currency devaluations and economic warfare for private gain no longer would threaten to wreak havoc with the economic system as a whole.

- Private pensions, savings, and investments would be secure.

- Social Security, Medicare, and Medicaid would be secure in perpetuity.

- Washington, the states and local communities could produce comfortable surpluses.

- Sustained prosperity overall would result, providing everyone with affordable or free healthcare, education, and other essential social benefits.

It's not pie-in-the-sky. The secret wasn't in issuing a lot of money. It lay in recycling money into local economies for productive growth without having to take on a debt burden for doing so. Wherever it's been tried, it's work impressively. Brown's *Web of Debt* explained it, but there are many others writing in this vein, for those who want to understand it better.[3]

Now's the time to change back by replacing the Federal Reserve's franchise with public banking, giving federal, state and local governments their own money system, to grow their areas and the nation sustainably and impressively, interest-free, with low or no taxes. This is what America has lacked for the last century.

Doing so would revolutionize the country en route perhaps to ending predatory capitalism entirely—with the ultimate aim of replacing a destructive system with an equitable one, and serving everyone fairly.

Why Public Banking is Needed

A new US census report offers more evidence why, saying one-fourth of US counties are dying (760 of 3,142), meaning they're showing more deaths than births, reflecting the deepening economic crisis causing record high unemployment, home foreclosures, and human misery. According to Professor Kenneth Johnson, "The downturn in the US economy is only exacerbating the problem. In some cases, the only thing that can pull an area out is an influx of young Hispanic immigrants or new economic development"[4]—which is not forthcoming.

University of Albany senior fellow James Follain said, "The housing (market decline) is creating a new type of ghost cities"[5] because of waves of foreclosures in overbuilt urban areas. Recovery will be very slow, he said, because of fiscal restraint when stimulus is badly needed.

Instead of curing the patient, we're killing it because giant banks control money, and government is colluding with them to wreck Main Stream America in order to create assets they can buy cheap at the expense of working households. That's how private money power works—for the wealthy, reaping hugely disproportionate rewards not by merit but by playing in a game rigged against the common good. What more incentive is there for returning money creation to public hands where it belongs, serving everyone equitably and fairly?

A Presently Existing Workable Model: The Bank of North Dakota

One state alone has public banking. North Dakota established the Bank of North Dakota (BND) in 1919. You can access its web site at http://www.banknd.nd.gov/.

In contrast to privatized banks, it's not insured by the Federal Deposit Insurance Corporation (FDIC) for good reason. Instead, its deposits "are guaranteed by the full faith and credit of the State of North Dakota," proved trustworthy after over 90 years of sound money practices, unlike banks trapped by Fed control, wrecking many over decades.

Its deposit base is also unique, comprised mainly of state residents and funds of state institutions. However, other deposits are accepted from any private or public source. As mandated in 1919, North Dakota's Industrial Commission oversees BND. Its members include the governor as chairman, the attorney general and the commissioner of agriculture. The bank also has a seven-member governor-appointed advisory board, knowledgeable in banking and finance.

On December 8, 2010, Governor Jack Dalrymple's 2011-2013 Budget Address highlighted a performance record other states struggling to cope with out-of-control deficits would envy. In contrast, North Dakota had surpluses throughout the economic crisis. As a result, it's budgeting "unprecedented funding for transportation infrastructure, housing, water supply and water control projects and other infrastructure investments throughout the state."

Greater funding will also go for K-12 and higher education, economic development, agricultural research, health and human services, as well as quality of life enhancements, and public worker pay increases. Not only that, there will be more for tax relief for state residents, amounting to $900 million in the 2011-2013 bienniums.

Moreover, strong reserves will be grown and maintained. Instead of cutting back like most other states, North Dakota is expanding and passing on benefits to residents. In December 2010, it also had the nation's lowest unemployment rate at 3.3%. BNB deserves the credit.

On January 4, Dalrymple delivered his State of the State Address, saying, "While other states [struggle with weak economies], we in North Dakota are in a position of strength and can use our surplus funds to meet the needs of the state" adequately, despite $174 million less federal human services aid than last year.

Despite the federal cutback, North Dakota is prosperous. "You can see it in the progress of our industries, our main streets, in our schools, and in our overall economic growth. Our progress is getting national attention. It's attracting people from other states and it's allowing [our] people to stay close to home."

North Dakota's impressive record includes:

- large budget surpluses;

- merchandise exports nearly doubled to $2 billion in the last five years alone;

- 40,000 new jobs added in the last decade while the nation lost them;

- the country's lowest unemployment rate at 3.3%; and

- much more revealing progress and prosperity, Dalrymple saying he's "fortunate today to be able to say with complete confidence that the state of our state is strong and growing stronger!" As a result, more impressive things are planned because North Dakota has resources to implement them, while other states cut back.

On February 20, 2011 the *Bismark Tribune* reported that "North Dakota's economy has been [producing] black gold, a $1 billion budget surplus, the nation's lowest unemployment," even though some residents need help. "It means there are still people, and families, who face a variety of challenges." As a result, state and local governments "have been proactive about" helping them get benefits they need and deserve. The state has plenty of resources to do it.

An October 12, 2010, a *Before It's News* headline said:

North Dakota Has A One Billion Dollar Budget Surplus
this year and is looking for ways to spend it—Maine has a
billion-dollar deficit and is looking for ways to fund it.

The subhead read:

North Dakota is the only state with a surplus. It is also

adding jobs when other states are losing them. Why is this not headline news?

North Dakota is not only solvent, it's thriving with impressive 43% personal income growth besides 34% more in total wages.

According to Brown, it's because BND has been a "credit machine," for over 90 years, delivering "sound financial services that promote agriculture, commerce and industry," something no other state can match because they don't have state-owned banks.

As a state-owned bank, BND "create[s] 'credit' with accounting entries on [its] books" through fractional reserve banking that multiplies each deposited amount magically about tenfold in the form of loans or computer-generated funds. As a result, the bank can re-lend many times over, and the more deposits, the greater amount available for sustained, productive growth. If all states owned public banks, they'd be as prosperous as North Dakota and be able to rebate taxes and expand public services, not extract more or cut them.

Brown explains that the BND "chiefly acts as a central bank, with functions similar to those of a branch of the Federal Reserve," which is neither federal nor has reserves as it's owned by major private banks in each of the 12 Fed districts. New York is by far the most dominant, with Wall Street majority control and a Fed chairman doing its bidding.

In contrast, BND is a public bank, 100% owned by the state, operating in the public interest and those of the state. It "avoids rivalry with private banks by partnering with them." Local banks do most lending. "The BND then comes in to participate in the loan, share risk, buy down the interest rate and buy up loans, thereby freeing up banks to lend more" as part of a continuing prosperity-creating virtuous circle. One of its functions "is to provide a secondary market for real estate loans, which it buys from local banks. Its residential loan portfolio is now $500 to $600 billion" in a state with around 700,000 people, and thriving.

BND's function in the property market helped it "avoid the credit crisis that afflicted Wall Street when the secondary market for loans collapsed in late 2007 and helped it reduce its foreclosure rate...[Its other services] include guarantees for entrepreneurial startups and student loans, the purchase of municipal bonds from public institutions, and a well-funded disaster loan program." When the state didn't meet its budget "a few years ago, the BND met the shortfall."

Year after year it works, freeing North Dakota from today's credit crisis and the worst of the economic downturn. It's a win-win for the state, its agriculture, commerce, industry, entrepreneurial startups, students, homebuyers needing loans, and virtually anyone in the state able to qualify.

In sum, state-owned banks have "enormous advantages over smaller private institutions...Their asset bases are not marred by oversized salaries and bonuses, they have no shareholders" demanding high returns, and they don't speculate in derivatives or other high-risk investments. As a result, BND is healthy with a 25% return on equity, paying "a hefty dividend to the state projected at over $60 million in 2009" and well over five times that amount in the last decade. This begs the question: why don't other states operate the same way? With state-owned banks, they might not be struggling the way nearly all of them are today, especially major ones like California, New York, Michigan and Illinois.

Growing State Interest in Public Banks

On March 25, 2011, Ellen Brown's article headlined, "A Choice for States: Banks, Not Budget Crises," highlighted the growing interest in state-owned banks, including new initiatives exploring the idea. There are at least 14 states so far with pending bills or feasibility studies to determine their potential. They include Oregon, Washington, Maryland, Illinois, Virginia, Massachusetts, Louisiana, California, Arizona, Maine, Vermont, New Mexico, New York and Hawaii—all considering public bank options like North Dakota's, America's most prosperous state.

At issue is the fact that while "Wall Street is [thriving], local banks are floundering, credit for small businesses and consumers remains tight, and local governments are teetering on bankruptcy." Congress is even considering new legislation to let states do it—as a way to avoid pension and other obligations. Yet, according to what's known, the Fed gave giant banks $12.3 trillion dollars, providing nothing for strapped states, local communities, and beleaguered households struggling to stay afloat.

North Dakota avoids economic hardships. So can other states and communities with publicly owned banks. It's not rocket science. It's simple. That's its beauty, and what works for North Dakota can work anywhere. Size isn't the issue. Policy is.

As a result, momentum's slowly building for change—in Illinois, for example, where on February 5, 2011, Rep. Mary Flowers introduced the Community Bank of Illinois Act,[6] which:

> Provides that the Department of Financial and Professional Regulation shall operate the Community Bank of Illinois. Specifies the authority of the advisory board of directors to the Bank. Provides that the Secretary is to employ a president and employees. Contains provisions concerning the removal and discharge of appointees. Provides that

State funds must be deposited in the Bank. Contains provisions concerning the nonliability of officers and sureties after deposit. Specifies the powers of the Bank.

Contains provisions concerning the guaranty of deposits and the Bank's role as a clearinghouse, the authorization of loans [to] the General Revenue Fund, bank loans to farmers, limitations on the loans by the Bank, the name in which business is conducted and titles taken, civil actions, surety on appeal, audits, electronic fund transfer systems, confidentiality of bank records, the sale and leasing of acquired agricultural real estate, and the illinois higher education savings plan.

Provides that the Bank is the custodian of securities. Amends the Illinois State Auditing Act to require that the Auditor General must contract with an independent certified accounting firm for an annual audit of the Community Bank of Illinois as provided in the Community Bank of Illinois Act. Amends the Eminent Domain Act to allow the Bank to acquire property by eminent domain.

In California, on May 2nd, 2011, Assembly Member Ben Hueso announced the hearing of AB 750, a "Bill Creating a Task Force to Consider Formation of a State Bank". Besides other provisions,

This bill would establish the investment blue ribbon task force to consider the viability of establishing the California Investment Trust, which would be a state bank receiving deposits of all state funds. The trust would support economic development, provide financing for housing development, public works and educational infrastructure, provide stability to the financial sector, provide state government banking services, lend capital to specified financial institutions, and provide for excess earnings of the trust to be used for state General Fund purposes.

The bill would establish the membership of the task force, which would include designated Members of the Legislature and designees of the Governor, Controller, and Treasurer...The bill would require the task force to report to the Legislature by December 1, 2012, on its findings and recommendations to the viability of establishing the California Investment Trust" and state-owned bank.[7]

In New York, on March 28, 2011, Assemblywoman Sandy Galef introduced Bill Number A6737, titled:

> An act to establish a commission to study the feasibility of establishing a bank owned by the state of New York or by a public authority constituted by the state of New York; and providing for the repeal of such provisions upon expiration thereof.

The bill's purpose is to establish a commission to study the feasibility of a state-owned bank and report back within two years.

Candidates in the November 2010 elections also proposed state banks in Florida, Idaho, Maine, Vermont, and Michigan, though legislation for them hasn't passed. In 2010, Michigan's bill got the most coverage. It calls a State of Michigan Development Bank an instrument to:

> provide credit worthy [state] Businesses loans and lines of credit on fair terms to protect and expand existing businesses and jobs, to attract new high technology and manufacturing businesses to Michigan, to put Michigan's skilled workforce to work, and provide needed credit for Michigan farm businesses and the important tourism industry.[8]

It proposed using some of the $58 billion from four Michigan pension funds as initial seed capital to launch it to help local businesses and create jobs. So far the measure has stalled without a legislative majority to pass it.

In the 19th century, Louisiana once had a state bank but liquidated it in 1908. Louisiana State Bank Records show the legislature created the Louisiana State Bank in March 1818 after the charter of the Louisiana Bank neared expiration.

At the time, the bank was endowed with $2 million in seed capital. Funded with $100,000, each of five branches operated autonomously. Besides providing capital for state agriculture, the bank also participated in financing the railroad industry in the mid-1800s.

It operated during Louisiana's unprecedented growth period, with state imports and exports rivaling most other states. In 1871, it became the State National Bank, then unfortunately it was liquidated 11 years before North Dakota's BND was established.

Perhaps its reemergence lies ahead.

Socially Responsible Banking **in Venezuela**

The website of the Banco Central de Venezuela (Venezuela's Central Bank) relates BCV history from its September 8, 1939 inception. At the time, conservative forces feared monetary instability under uncontrolled Central Bank spending. As a result, opponents (unsuccessfully) said giving it exclusive money creation power was unconstitutional.

Thereafter eight BCV reforms occurred between 1943 and 2001. In 2010, banking was made a "public service". More on that below.

In 1992, legislation established "administrative autonomy," in part transforming the bank into a "public legal entity. Until then, [it was solely] corporate in nature." Thereafter, Venezuela's president appointed "a collegiate body of seven members, a president and six directors," requiring two-thirds Senate approval for a six-year term. Its mandate is "monetary stability, economic balance and well-ordered economic development."

Under Article 156 (11) of Venezuela's 1999 Constitution, National Public Power controls:

> Regulation of central banking, the monetary system, foreign currency, the financial and capital market system and the issuance and mintage of currency.

Section Three: National Monetary System, Article 318, states:

> The monetary competence of National Authority shall necessarily be exercised exclusively by the Venezuelan Central Bank (BCV). [Its] fundamental objective...is to achieve price stability and preserve the internal and foreign exchange value of the monetary unit...The Venezuelan Central Bank is a public-law juridical person with autonomy to formulate and implement policies within its sphere of competence.

Article 319 says it "shall be governed by the principle of public responsibility." Failure to do so "shall result in removal of the Board of Directors...[It] shall be subject to oversight by the Office of the General Comptroller of the Republic..."

Under Venezuela's 2010 Organic Law on the Domestic Financial System, banks, insurance companies, brokerage firms, and other financial institutions "have the obligation of collaborating with sectors of the productive, popular communal economy through healthy financial intermediation, inspired by the spirit of productive transformation."

In other words, their mandate includes funding traditional economic sectors as well as social and communal production entities and related organizations. In addition, advancing collective savings and promoting alternative communal investments is required.

Moreover, a recent amendment of the Law of the Central Bank of Venezuela abolished its autonomy, mandating a new financial structure to include adapting its "legal, administrative and functional structure to the goals of the production model, and the Central Bank may not be detached from the actual needs of the economy."

BCV operations must also conform to the National Development Plan "to meet the objectives of a socialist state," even though Venezuela's economy is more private than public. The amended law, however, states that "changes shall be construed as part of a progressive and timely reform to the financial system and as an opportunity to enhance the role of the institution in the transformation process of the social production model."

Venezuelan Banking: A Public Service

On December 20, 2010, Venezuela Analysis contributor Juan Reardon headlined, "Venezuelan National Assembly Passes Law Making Banking a 'Public Service,'"[9] saying the new law, approved on December 19, 2010, defines banking as a public service, required "to contribute more to social programs, housing construction efforts, and other social needs while making government intervention easier when banks fail to comply with national priorities."

Formerly called the Law of Banking Sector Institutions, the new measure "protects bank customers' assets" from owner irregularities. It also prohibits banking hour changes, and mandates the Superintendent of Banking Institutions to serve the interests of customers as well as owners.

United Socialist Party (PSUV) legislator Ricardo Sanguino called it necessary "to consolidate a responsible financial sector," which is entirely absent in America where giant banks are more predators than responsible financial institutions. Sanguino said Venezuela's new law "restrict[s] unregulated speculation. [Now] there is absolutely no chance that a banking institution becomes involved in irregularities," as happened previously.

Speculation now will be controlled by limiting the credit amount to individuals or private entities to "20% [of the] maximum amount of capital a bank can have out...Commercial banks, insurance companies, investment banks, and brokerage firms must also operate" separately, unlike in America where they operate without restraint.

Further, 5% of pre-tax bank profits must be used solely for communal council projects, and 10% of bank capital for a fund "to pay wages and pensions in case of bankruptcy."

While the new measure doesn't suggest full banking nationalization ahead, it does mean the government must act responsibly to secure the system for all Venezuelans, not solely for powerful capital interests as in America. Though many companies, including banks, have been nationalized in the last decade, "private banks still play a majority role [with] roughly 70% of assets."

Other Banking Reforms

In August 2010, the National Assembly reformed the Bank Law, prohibiting owners, directors, and administrators of media or telecommunication companies from managing banks. Its purpose is to prevent information manipulation, including deceptive offers and other types of fraud, benefitting them at the expense of ordinary citizens.

It also clarified which institutions are affected. As a result, Sudeban (the Superintendency of Banks and other Financial Institutions) will require Sovereign People's Bank (BPS) to provide more communal services by facilitating deposits, withdrawals, savings, and credit issuance. BPS was founded in 1999 to fight poverty by offering non-financial services, like training and micro-financing, to communities, small companies, and cooperatives, sectors private banks often ignored.

Venezuela's Bolivarian Spirit

Count on opposition lawmakers, hostile US ones, Venezuela's right-wing media, and its US counterparts to use any opportunity to bash Chavez and Bolivarianism. The same drumbeat now echoes about its banking and other reforms. They're largely absent in big money-run America where Wall Street and other corporate predators exploit investors and working households.

in contrast, a Bolivarian spirit governs Venezuela. Still developing, it freed the country from what Bolivar called the imperial curse that "plague[d] Latin America with misery in the name of liberty."

Public service banking strengthens social democracy, unlike in America where Wall Street's stranglehold on public wealth enables self-interested profiteering, the curse of working households.

The Public Banking Institute: Banking in the Public Interest

Ellen Brown heads an initiative to promote this idea whose time has come, explaining that public banks are:

- viable economic solutions to promote sustainable growth and prosperity;

- available to states, cities and local communities of any size;

- owned and operated by states or local communities, not private investors, scamming the system for profit at the public's expense;

- economically viable like private banks, but more stable and secure;

- "able to offset tax increases with returned credit income to" communities;

- ready resources for state and local governments, "eliminating the need for large 'rainy day' funds," sitting dormant and unused;

- help for local businesses, farmers, working households and students, not casinos to speculate recklessly like private banks; and

- legal according to the Supreme Court.

In contrast, public banks aren't:

- run by politicians, but by bankers responsible to states, local communities and the public welfare;

- "boondoggles for bank executives; rather, their employees are salaried public servants [paid by states or local governments with transparent pay structures] who [won't likely] earn bonuses, commissions or fees for generating loans;" or

- "speculative ventures that maximize [short-term] profits without regard to the long-term" public interest, what responsible banking is supposed to stress.

Overall, public banks differ from private ones by being mandated to serve the public interest, not shareholders or corporate executives seeking maximum profits for personal gain. Moreover, by returning the profits generated, lower taxes and interest rates are possible. In addition, by not needing to pay themselves interest, state project costs can, on average, be reduced by 50%.

In short, public banks work, serving people responsibly, unlike greedy bankers, ripping them off for personal gain. The time for change is now. The way forward: public banks serving all Americans equitably and fairly for sustainable long-term growth and prosperity.

Besides peace, good will, democratic values, and equity and justice for all, what better idea is there than that?

Endnotes

1   Michael Hudson, "Obama's Awful Financial Recovery Plan," *Counterpunch*, February 12, 2009, available at <http://www.counterpunch.org/hudson02122009.html>

2   Ellen Brown, *Web of Debt*, Third Millennium Press, fourth edition 2010.

3   See Stephen Zarlenga, *The Lost Science of Money: The Mythology of Money, The Story of Power,*American Monetary Institute, December 2007.

4   Cited in Hope Yen and John Raby, "Census: Near Record Level of US Counties Dying," Associated Press, February 22, 2011.

5   International Business News, "One in 4 US Cities Dying: Census Bureau", February 22, 2011.

6   Available at <http://www.housedem.state.il.us/members/flowersm/billspon.htm>

7   Available at <http://asmdc.org/members/a79/press-releases/item/2641-assembly-committee-votes-on-bill-creating-task-force-to-consider-formation-of-state-bank>

8   Available at <http://jobs4michigan.org/index.php?option=com_content&view=article&id=2&Itemid=3>

9   Available at <http://venezuelanalysis.com/news/5880>

INDEX